Praise for *ReNew*

I am very excited for the release of this book, as there are multitudes of people who will be helped and strengthened by the content of *ReNew*. I love that Julie Winter addresses both natural and supernatural realms. These areas blend beautifully together in the life well lived. She provides us with brilliant insight, biblical perspectives, sound medical counsel, and practical suggestions that should help and inspire every reader. Read, be encouraged, and be strengthened by stepping into your God-given inheritance called health and joy.

BILL JOHNSON
Bethel Church, Redding, CA
Author of *The Supernatural Power of the Transformed Mind*
and *God is Good*

Julie Winter is a highly respected medical professional who is also paying close attention to the whole person. Her compassionate work with patients to address emotional, spiritual, and physical needs creates a steady stream of wellness in her practice. Her successful interventions are now accessible in this journey called *ReNew*. *ReNew* is a precious resource for those who struggle with the stress of anxiety and depression. I highly recommend this book to those who want freedom and understanding from this debilitating and disruptive condition.

DANNY SILK
President of Loving on Purpose
Bestselling author of *Loving Our Kids on Purpose*,
Culture of Honor, and *Keep Your Love On*

D1510988

Julie Winter's book, *ReNew*, will show you how to take action towards optimal mental health. In psychiatry, the goal of treatment is "recovery," but by integrating steps toward renewal of the mind in Christ, this book provides a vision of mental wellness that is whole and accessible without a co-payment for the appointment (Christ already paid the fee). As an adjunct to professional treatment, *ReNew* empowers the individual who's serious about inviting God into the treatment plan. With book in hand, we each have an opportunity to participate with God as He advances His Kingdom on Earth as it is in Heaven. Whether you read this yourself or share it with others in need of renewal of their minds, I pray many will be blessed through the words between the pages.

Renewed and a conduit in Christ,

DEBORAH JOHNSON, MSN, APRN, PMHNP-BC
Associate Health Sciences Clinical Professor
UCSF School of Nursing, Community Health Systems

ReNew

BREAKING FREE FROM NEGATIVE THINKING, ANXIETY, AND DEPRESSION

JULIE WINTER

© Copyright 2017–Julie Winter

All rights reserved. This book is protected by the copyright laws of the United States of America. This book may not be copied or reprinted for commercial gain or profit. The use of short quotations or occasional page copying for personal or group study is permitted and encouraged. Permission will be granted upon request. Unless otherwise identified, Scripture quotations are taken from the HOLY BIBLE, NEW INTERNATIONAL VERSION®, Copyright © 1973, 1978, 1984, 2011 International Bible Society. Used by permission of Zondervan. All rights reserved. Scripture quotations marked ESV are taken from The Holy Bible, English Standard Version® (ESV®), copyright © 2001 by Crossway, a publishing ministry of Good News Publishers. Used by permission. All rights reserved. Scripture quotations marked KJV are taken from the King James Version. Scripture quotations marked NKJV are taken from the New King James Version. Copyright © 1982 by Thomas Nelson, Inc. Used by permission. All rights reserved. Scripture quotations marked NLT are taken from the Holy Bible, New Living Translation, copyright 1996, 2004. Used by permission of Tyndale House Publishers., Wheaton, Illinois 60189. All rights reserved. Scripture quotations marked NASB are taken from the NEW AMERICAN STANDARD BIBLE®, Copyright © 1960, 1962, 1963, 1968, 1971, 1972, 1973, 1975, 1977, 1995 by The Lockman Foundation. Used by permission. All emphasis within Scripture quotations is the author's own.

DESTINY IMAGE® PUBLISHERS, INC.

P.O. Box 310, Shippensburg, PA 17257-0310

"Promoting Inspired Lives."

This book and all other Destiny Image and Destiny Image Fiction books are available at Christian bookstores and distributors worldwide.

Cover design by Eileen Rockwell

Interior design by Terry Clifton

For more information on foreign distributors, call 717-532-3040.

Reach us on the Internet: www.destinyimage.com.

ISBN 13 TP: 978-0-7684-1222-2

ISBN 13 eBook: 978-0-7684-1223-9

ISBN HC: 978-0-7684-1558-2

ISBN LP: 978-0-7684-1559-9

For Worldwide Distribution, Printed in the U.S.A.

1 2 3 4 5 6 7 8 / 21 20 19 18 17

I dedicate this book to my patients, many of whom have suffered untold trauma, abuse, hardship, and deprivation to seek a life of freedom. Their courage in adversity inspires me to bring freedom to others. I also dedicate this book to my loving husband, who has encouraged me to finish this work, even though it meant time spent away from him.

Acknowledgments

To my friend, Andre Van Mol, MD, who not only encouraged me but spent hours reviewing and editing each chapter for accuracy. Thank you, Andre, your time and love means the world to me.

To my mom, Zola Cusick, a retired teacher and lover of grammar. She faithfully read and edited each chapter. Mom, you have loved me and inspired me to be excellent, faithful, and go for the impossible. I only hope that I can be as good a teacher as you.

To my dad, Orvan Cusick, who is the best father ever. Your example of faithfulness to your family and God, your work ethic and love of family has profoundly shaped the person I am today. Your love, encouragement, and courage mean everything to me.

To my sons, Zachary and Adrian, I am so proud of you. Your love for family and God, your work ethic, your integrity, and your faithfulness inspires me more than you know.

Contents

Foreword

In 2008, my family went through a terrible crisis that lasted more than two years. In the midst of trying to help my family weather the storm, I found myself in my own personal battle for survival. What began as a couple of months of sleepless nights soon became a full-on emotional breakdown.

I laid on my couch in a deep depression for six months; every day was a living hell. Day after day, my friend and personal nurse practitioner, Julie Winter, called to encourage and counsel me. Slowly but surely I began to improve, and about a year later I finally, fully recovered.

I have discovered that a lot of professionals have different theories about how to restore people. Many of them focus their treatment on the body or the soul. But Julie has a unique and holistic approach to restoring broken people. She develops a tridimensional plan—spirit, soul, and body, for each of her patients. Instead of just treating symptoms and creating symptomatic cures, Julie actually treats the root causes of each person's brokenness.

I was so impressed by Julie's approach to wholeness and the effects it had on my own life, that I all but begged her to write a book about it. I am really excited about this book. I know thousands of people who are suffering from depression, anxiety, panic attacks, insomnia, etc. will be restored by the insights in this manuscript.

Consequently, Julie's book, *ReNew*, is more than a book. It's a road back to recovery and a compass to wholeness. If you, or someone you love is suffering from these symptoms, this book, *ReNew*, is for you. It will change your life.

KRIS VALLOTTON

Senior Associate Leader, Bethel Church, Redding, CA

Co-Founder of Bethel School of Supernatural Ministry

Author of eleven books, including *The Supernatural Ways of Royalty* and *Spirit Wars*.

Introduction

At the prompting of my dear husband and the urging of both patients and friends, I began to formulate ideas for a book that would help people change the way they perceive anxiety and depression and to break off the guilt of pursuing treatment. Many people are ashamed and they suffer needlessly, in silence.

The Kingdom of God is righteousness, peace, and joy, the opposite of depression and anxiety. Joy and peace should be the normal state of those who are in Christ Jesus. For many, this is only a theoretical concept that applies to others The purpose of this book is to outline practical steps to make joy and peace obtainable.

Anxiety and depression are prevalent conditions in our society, both inside and outside the church. There is a tremendous lack of understanding about the physical chemistry of our brain and a false perception that it's just "mind over matter" or "I just need to pray more and I will get better."

I want to be clear that I do not have a degree in psychology or counseling. I received a master's degree in nursing from the UCLA Family

Nurse Practitioner program in 1987. Unfortunately, the funding for much of the mental health services in California has disappeared. Many of the patients I used to refer to psychiatry I now treat, as mental health providers are scarce. Most family physicians, nurse practitioners, and physician's assistants treat complex psychiatric patients simply because there is no one else available. These tools were developed out of years of working with people who were stuck in anxiety and depression.

The emphasis of this book is focused toward treatment of generalized anxiety disorder and mild to moderate depression. Although these tools may be useful for obsessive compulsive disorder, panic disorder, bipolar depression, and severe major depressive disorder, medications, and counseling will be indicated as well. These conditions are associated with major physical changes in the brain and are beyond the scope of this book.

I have been a family nurse practitioner for many years and have had the wonderful privilege of caring for people of all ages and from all socioeconomic backgrounds. In the last twenty years, we have made profound advances in the medical management of anxiety and depression. This has completely changed the way we treat these conditions, giving hope and improved quality of life to many who had not responded to previous treatment modalities. Increased understanding of how the brain works and medications that specifically target neurotransmitter sites have given the medical community more tools to help people function better in their family and work relationships. Also, it is more acceptable in our society to admit we struggle with mood disorders. People now seek help, where in years past they would have lived their entire lives anxious or depressed because there were no other options. Fortunately, increased treatment options and social acceptability have caused more people to seek care. Treatment of mood disorders has become a very large part of what I treat today, accounting for close to 20 percent of my practice.

The purpose of this book is to help you understand what happens in your body, mind, and spirit when you are anxious or depressed and outline some practical strategies that will help you discover peace and joy as a lifestyle. Happiness is truly an inside job.

The format of this book defines the physical, psychological, and spiritual components of depression, describes what's in a thought, and outlines some practical tools for both prevention and treatment of anxiety and depression. Jesus is our model and He expressed a perfect and practical theology. Everyone would agree that Jesus managed His spiritual life perfectly—living a life of worship and praise to the Father. However, Jesus also gave us the model for stewarding our physical body and our thought life. This perfect expression of stewarding all three areas well is the theme that runs throughout this book.

There are numerous stories sprinkled throughout that reflect many years of practice. I have been careful to change the names and certain identifying factors to maintain patient privacy.

Although the tools are universal and can be used by anyone suffering from anxiety or depression, I have targeted the Christian community as this group suffers tremendous guilt for seeking help in overcoming anxiety and depression. There are persistent misperceptions about mood disorders in the Body of Christ, and my hope is that this book dispels the myths and gives people permission to seek treatment.

We were created in God's image and were designed to live a life of joy. The Kingdom of God is righteousness, peace, and joy, and this is the inheritance of all who believe. Take heart. Anxiety and depression do not belong to you. Now is the time for freedom.

Do not conform to the pattern of this world, but be transformed by the renewing of your mind (Romans 12:2).

Chapter 1

———

Joy

"Joy runs deeper than despair."
—CORRIE TEN BOOM

T he purpose of this book is to provide practical tools to those struggling with anxiety and depression. But before we talk about mood
disorders, I want to make a strong case for joy, the normal mood for every
follower of Jesus, no matter the circumstances. This is not to negate the
fact that we all experience sadness, anger, grief, or other negative emotions, but these negative emotions should be temporary, not our normal
state of being.

Did you know that joy is the hallmark, the sign of a true believer?
Paul writes:

For the kingdom of God is not a matter of eating and drinking, but of righteousness, peace and joy in the Holy Spirit (Romans 14:17).

As my friend and pastor, Kris Vallotton, says, "Two thirds of the kingdom is felt." If we truly live in the Kingdom, under the domain of King Jesus, then we reside under the ruling atmosphere of our king. Jesus is full of joy, peace, love, faith, mercy, kindness, and everything that is good. All that is in Him is available to us. Joy and peace are the inheritance of the believer, and not for just our future state in Heaven but for our current state as well.

Fear, depression, anxiety, bitterness, anger, hatred, envy, etc. are not rooted in the Kingdom of God. These negative emotions originate and flow from the ruler of another kingdom, a kingdom that we have authority over through Jesus Christ. These negative emotions should be foreign to us, not familiar, normal, or frequent. When these negative thoughts and emotions arise in our soul, we need to realize quickly which kingdom is trying to influence us. It is our responsibility to use the weapons and armor given to us by our Father. We always, and I mean always, have access to a greater Kingdom, and we have authority over these negative thoughts. That is why John could write:

You, dear children, are from God and have overcome them, because the one who is in you is greater than the one who is in the world (1 John 4:4).

The king we serve is the King of kings and the Lord of lords and in Him is great joy. Jesus Himself said:

As the Father has loved me, so have I loved you. Now remain in my love. If you keep my commands, you will remain in my love, just as I have kept my Father's commands and remain in his love. I have told you this so that my joy may be in you and that your joy may be complete (John 15:9-11).

Joy is truly the normal state of the believer. If you do not arise each morning with a sense of joy and peace in your heart, then something is wrong in your spirit. I liken fear or depression to fever, which is a symptom of an underlying disease. When you develop a fever, you know your body is fighting an infection. You may treat the fever with aspirin for a few days, but if it persists you will probably go see your medical provider to find the cause. In other words, you understand that even though you can bring the fever down with medication, the fever is a symptom of something more serious that needs attention.

Yet how often do we experience feelings of fear, anxiety, dread, sadness, and other negative emotions and just assume that this is normal or okay? We don't see these negative emotions as symptoms of an underlying disease in our body, mind, or spirit. Some of us have become so familiar with these negative thought patterns that they have become normal. Joy and peace have become feelings that are infrequent and fleeting, instead of the other way around.

Do you expect to awaken each day with a sense of peace and joy? You should because joy is normal. Anything else indicates underlying illness in your being.

Not swayed by circumstances in life or the world around us, we know that Christ lives in us and that He loves us beyond all measure and reason. Joy is not an occasional feeling or a promise for the future but our core, the place we live from daily. This is the reason Paul said:

Rejoice in the Lord always. I will say it again: Rejoice! (Philippians 4:4)

Do you understand that the joy of the Lord is your strength? Joy can be a stronghold in your life if you learn how to cultivate joy as a lifestyle.

> *Being strengthened with all power, according to his glorious might, for all endurance and patience with joy, giving thanks to the Father, who has qualified you to share in the inheritance of the saints in light* (Colossians 1:11-12 ESV).

I want to give you permission to be joyful. Many people feel guilty when they experience joy. It is true that there is sorrow and tragedy in our world, and sometimes we feel guilty for feeling joyful when we know others are sad. Yet it is healthy to focus on what is good and right in the world around us, to train our mind to meditate on all that Christ has accomplished for us. Not only is it our right, but it is our duty to live a life of joy. Anything else inaccurately displays the Kingdom.

Think about it. Don't you enjoy being around people who are cheerful and joyful? I have numerous patients who, no matter their illness, always have a joyful, hopeful spirit. I can think of one particular patient who always comes in with a smile and a kind word. Tracy is the caretaker of her disabled husband, and she has several serious medical conditions herself. As her husband is unable to work, she works full time to provide for her family. This woman has every reason in the world to be depressed and worried, but she is always so cheerful, hopeful, and thankful to God. She looks at her world and purposefully finds what is good, then focuses her attention there.

In comparison, Norman, an older gentleman, lives in a constant state of anxiety. Peace and joy are rare experiences for him. The physical and psychological effects of anxiety drive people to seek medical care more often than people who are not anxious or depressed, so I've gotten to know Norman quite well. He has a wonderful wife and children, good health, and stable finances. But instead of being thankful for what he has, he focuses on what is wrong in the world around him. He has not mastered the instructions given to us by Paul:

Whatever is true, whatever is noble, whatever is right, whatever is pure, whatever is lovely, whatever is admirable—if anything is excellent or praiseworthy—think about such things…. And the God of peace will be with you (Philippians 4:8-9).

Joy awaits this man. It is there for the taking because joy is a choice that is not dependent on circumstances. Norman is in better health and financially more stable than Tracy. If anyone had a right to worry, it would be Tracy. The difference is that she has set her mind to trust in God. She is thankful and looks for the good around her. You do find what you are looking for. If you look for good things, you will find them. If you look for bad things, you will find them. What are you looking for?

Be joyful always? Really? Can you be joyful when your children are not living for God or when you are facing bankruptcy? Can you be joyful when you look at what is happening in our government, the economy, or the world around us? What about a diagnosis of cancer or loss of a job? Is there a place of joy for you there? The answer is a resounding yes!

Be joyful in hope, patient in affliction, faithful in prayer (Romans 12:12).

I am not saying to pretend that everything is wonderful or to ignore evil. But these things do not have the power to rob us of our internal joy. Even when we face an impossible situation, we can *consider* it *joy,* as James said:

Consider it pure joy, my brothers and sisters, whenever you face trials of many kinds (James 1:2).

Jesus, our model for life, had quite a bit to say about joy.

These things I have spoken to you, that my joy may be in you, and that your joy may be full (John 15:11 ESV).

What would it look like to have the joy of Jesus filling your spirit, mind, and body in fullness? Do you comprehend the fullness of the joy of Christ dwelling in you?

The only way we can lose our joy is if we lose sight of our identity. Seriously. Can you even grasp how much you have in Christ right now? When I read the first two chapters of Ephesians, my heart explodes with joy, even though I am unable to comprehend fully the immensity of what Paul is trying to convey in this letter. My spirit understands, even though my mind is unable to grasp what it means to have every spiritual blessing, to be chosen before the creation of the world, to be holy and blameless, to be lavished with the riches of God's grace, to be made alive in Christ and seated with Him in heavenly places (currently, not just in the age to come). The only way I can not respond with great joy is to refuse to believe this is true for me.

Joy and peace are also fruits of the spirit? Paul states:

> *But the fruit of the Spirit is love, joy, peace, forbearance, kindness, goodness, faithfulness, gentleness and self-control* (Galatians 5:22-23).

Paul then goes on to say that if we live by the Spirit, we need to walk in step with the Spirit. Because the Kingdom of God is our inheritance, joy, along with righteousness and peace, belongs to us. The people in the world around us should know us for our joy. Do you exhibit enough peace and joy to convince the people around you who are from another kingdom?

I see so many anxious, fretful, and unhappy Christians in the world today. How can this be? This negative fruit comes from another tree and is foreign to the Holy Spirit. When we are robbed of our joy and peace, we are also robbed of our witness. Paul asked:

> *Where is that joyful and grateful spirit you felt then?* (Galatians 4:15 NLT)

We owe the world joy because it speaks of another kingdom within us, more powerful than our current circumstances. Jesus is the good news, the "tidings of great joy, to all people" and He lives in us (see Luke 2:10).

The peace and joy we carry is both superior and transferable. Joy sets us apart, marking us and making us an attractive fragrance to the world around us. We carry within us the ability to change the atmosphere of our surrounding environment. For many, the only God people will ever see is the God who lives in us. Paul states:

> To them God has chosen to make known among the Gentiles the glorious riches of this mystery, which is Christ in you, the hope of glory (Colossians 1:27).

How big is Christ in you? Does the peace of God that surpasses all understanding reside in you? It must. Not only is it your right and your inheritance, but you owe the people around you a model of our glorious and loving Savior, who is the Prince of Peace.

If you are in a difficult situation and put your trust in God, then you have a right to be full of joy in spite of your circumstances. Joy in the Lord protects you. You have the favor of the Lord as a shield.

> But let all who take refuge in you be glad; let them ever sing for joy. Spread your protection over them, that those who love your name may rejoice in you. Surely, Lord, you bless the righteous; you surround them with your favor as with a shield (Psalm 5:11-12).

Joy and peace are your rightful inheritance now and in the age to come. Make sure you do not let the enemy rob you of what belongs to you every day.

ACTION POINTS

If joy is not your normal state of being then read and meditate on the following Scriptures until they penetrate your spirit as truth.

- Psalms 16:11
- Psalms 126:5
- Isaiah 12:3
- Jeremiah 15:16
- John 15:11; 16:22-24
- Philippians 4:4
- Colossians 1:11-12
- Acts 20:24
- Romans 14:17
- James 1:2

1. Is joy my default state? If not, what robs me of my joy?

_____

_____

_____

_____

2. What does God say about my situation?

_____

_____

_____

_____

3. What can I rejoice in daily, so that joy and peace are exhibited in my life every day?

_____

_____

_____

_____

_____

Chapter 2

What Is in a Thought?

"The happiness of your life depends
upon the quality of your thoughts."
—Marcus Aurelius

S o how do you move yourself from a state of anxiety and depression into a place of peace and joy? How do peace and joy become your normal state of being? Peace, joy, hope, gratitude, love, and other positive feelings or emotions are the *fruits* of our thoughts. It is the principle of cause and effect. This may sound simple, but good thoughts bring about feelings of love, hope, courage, joy, etc., and negative thoughts bring about fear, anger, hopelessness, sadness, etc. Thoughts produce feelings that produce an action or in some cases inaction.

Bryce, a 44-year-old gentleman, came in to see me due to recurrent depression. He told me that he felt fearful. Even though he had no proof, he suspected people were talking about him at work. These feelings caused him to interact with his co-workers by either shutting down (inaction) or behaving in a defensive manner (negative action). Bryce knew this wasn't logical as his work performance was good. I asked him what made him "feel" this way, i.e. what were the thoughts that generated these feelings. He admitted to thoughts of inadequacy and failure, even though there were no known problems at work. Bryce's negative thinking generated feelings of fear resulting in negative actions.

People judge us by our actions, as they do not know our thoughts or feelings. However, God has a much higher standard. He judges not just our actions, but the underlying thoughts as well. Jesus said:

> *You have heard that it was said, "You shall not commit adultery." But I tell you that anyone who looks at a woman lustfully has already committed adultery with her in his heart* (Matthew 5:27-28).

Let me point out that attempting to control feelings directly is ineffective. You cannot tell yourself to stop feeling a certain way. You have to change the thoughts that produce the feelings. This is why Paul did not say, "Take every feeling captive." Sometimes it takes a while for feelings to subside.

Panic attacks, which are characterized by overwhelming feelings of anxiety, leave a chemical effect that may last several hours, even when the initial trigger has resolved. After a panic attack, people often feel tired or wrung out because of the side effects of adrenaline. It is important to set your mind on the truth and take your thoughts captive regardless of feelings. Your feelings will eventually come into line with your thoughts.

Before I discuss helpful keys to renewed thinking, I want to describe anxiety and depression and explain what happens inside the brain when we think. It is vital to remember that the brain is an organ. And like other organs in our body, the brain is susceptible to dysfunction and damage when injured, which can result in abnormal electrical or chemical activity.

All anxiety and depressive disorders are not the same. They often coexist, but it is important to distinguish the type, as treatment will vary. Anxiety and depressive disorders are outlined more thoroughly in resources such as the *Diagnostic Statistical Manual of Mental Disorders* (DSM-IV).[1] There are several recognized subtypes of depression such as major depressive disorder (MDD), seasonal affective disorder, postpartum depression, bipolar disorder, and dysthymia, to name a few. Anxiety is also a spectrum of disorders, such as generalized anxiety disorder (GAD), panic disorder, obsessive-compulsive disorder, post-traumatic stress disorder, and others.

For the purposes of this book, I will discuss anxiety and depression in general terms. However, I do want to reiterate the fact that not all anxiety and depressive disorders are the same. They have different root causes, and treatment varies depending on the severity and type.

ANXIETY

Although these are separate disorders, anxiety and depression often coexist. Anxiety affects 40 million adults in the United States or about 12 percent of the population and is twice as likely to occur in women as compared to men. The average age of onset is in the twenties, but many of my patients tell me they can remember feeling anxious for much of their childhood. These people frequently have a family history of anxiety or depression.

People with anxiety disorders tend to seek more medical care and diagnostic testing than the general population. Anxiety produces worrisome symptoms such as feelings of fear or panic, racing or circling thoughts, difficulty concentrating, fatigue, irritability, insomnia, palpitations, dizziness, muscle tension, shortness of breath, numbness or tingling of the extremities, and stomach upset. As anxious patients are often quite intelligent and have creative imaginations, they worry about having a serious underlying disease and seek medical care for reassurance.

Lynn, who was in her mid-twenties, came in to see me several times for palpitations and dizziness. Her anxiety had triggered high blood pressure with subsequent visits to the emergency room. Her previous doctor had put her on a blood pressure medication, but Lynn was convinced that something else was wrong. She was worried that her high blood pressure was going to give her a heart attack or a stroke. This patient spent a great deal of time on the Internet researching her symptoms, which only increased her anxiety. Lynn came into the office with questions about very unlikely medical diagnoses. After several visits and repeatedly normal testing, I was finally able to convince Lynn that her underlying problem was anxiety. I explained how anxiety was a chemical reaction in her body that affected her physically, causing her to have insomnia and elevated blood pressure. As we treated her anxiety, she began to improve, and her blood pressure normalized. Within a couple of months, Lynn was able to stop the blood pressure medication.

Anxiety is triggered when a physical pathway in the brain is activated that prepares you to respond to danger. This chemical cascade is initiated in the amygdala, a portion of your brain that prepares you for the fight-or-flight response. This reaction occurs very quickly and can be helpful when you need adrenaline. For example, if you need to run across a busy intersection, a sense of danger will put some speed in your step. If you need to defend yourself from an attacker, the chemicals released into your body will give you additional strength and will temporarily reduce your sensitivity to pain. Skilled athletes and performers learn how to use adrenaline to their advantage.

Uncontrolled adrenaline is another matter altogether. Do you remember a time when you performed poorly on a test, stumbled through a speech, or forgot your lines in a play due to feeling overwhelmed with anxiety? Unchecked, adrenaline can cut off access to memories and logical thought processes. This is the reason panicked people may not make good decisions, and explains why you may have scored poorly on test material you knew quite well.

Unfortunately, your brain cannot distinguish between real and imaginary threats. The same adrenaline pathway is activated whether your home is being invaded or if you think about your home being invaded. The chemicals that help you run from an attacker aren't so helpful when you lie down at night, your thoughts circling like a merry-go-round as you imagine potential negative scenarios at work or home.

The operative word is *imagine*. When we imagine *what if* scenarios, our brain responds as if the threat were happening right now. Your husband is unexpectedly late from work, and you begin to wonder what could have happened to him. If you allow yourself, you can dream up all sorts of possible reasons why he is late. What if he had a flat tire? What if it's worse than that? What if he was in a car accident? Maybe he was seriously injured? Should you go look for him? What would you do if he died? Within a few seconds your imagination has led you down a pathway of an extremely threatening scenario; adrenaline is coursing through your body because your brain is unable to differentiate between reality and imagination. Your heart is beating fast as blood is shunted to your extremities preparing you to run or fight. Several minutes later your husband walks through the door, but it may take you more than an hour to overcome the after-effects of the adrenaline surge brought about by thoughts gone awry. This type of negative thought pattern can lead to chronic anxiety, which is quite destructive. Jesus made it quite clear that we are not to worry:

Peace I leave with you; my peace I give you. I do not give to you as the world gives. Do not let your hearts be troubled and do not be afraid (John 14:27).

Not only is anxiety a miserable state, it is unhealthy. Anxiety can cause stomach ulcers, elevated blood pressure, insomnia, headaches, depression, and substance abuse, as well as other illnesses.

People who suffer from chronic anxiety often feel anxious when there is no perceivable threat. In fact, when I ask my anxious patients what they're worried about, they often tell me they don't know. They express their frustration with how illogical it is for them to feel anxious, yet they feel powerless to change their thinking. People who suffer from chronic anxiety are not worried about a specific event such as a scheduled surgery or an upcoming court case. Their worry is more global and primarily centers on events that are unlikely to occur. As they imagine all of the possible things that could go wrong, they become overwhelmed, feeling powerless to change the outcomes of these imagined scenarios. Even though my patients realize their response is unwarranted, they don't know how to turn it off.

However, the truth is that we can renew our minds daily, and we can take our thoughts captive. Paul said:

Casting down imaginations, and every high thing that exalteth itself against the knowledge of God, and bringing into captivity every thought to the obedience of Christ (2 Corinthians 10:5 KJV).

I will talk about some specific strategies to renew your mind later on, but before I do that let me briefly discuss depression. Many people who suffer from anxiety are at risk for depression, and the reverse is true as well.

DEPRESSION

Depression is characterized by persistent feelings of sadness, which may manifest as feelings of hopelessness, helplessness, or worthlessness that affect one's ability to work and function. There may be difficulty with motivation, memory, concentration, and cognition. Other symptoms include changes in appetite or weight, difficulty sleeping, irritability, loss of interest in sex or usual pleasurable activities, fatigue, and thoughts of death or suicide.

According to the National Institute of Mental Health, the 2005 National Comorbidity Survey-Replication study reported that 9.5 percent of the population (20.9 million American adults) suffers from mood disorders.[2] Similar to anxiety disorders, women are twice as likely to suffer from depression compared to men.

Depression is a serious condition. Not only is it miserable for those suffering feelings of sadness, but depression is associated with an overall shorter life expectancy. Obviously, depressed people are more at risk for suicide, but depressed people are also more at risk for heart disease and substance abuse.

Carla, a lovely 23-year-old woman, came into my office, her face tight and eyes downcast. She told me that she woke up every morning with a sense of dread. She wanted to just pull the covers over her head and disappear. Carla had been calling in sick to work, was avoiding family and friends, and no longer liked to shop or go outdoors. What finally brought her in to see me were the fearful thoughts of not wanting to live. She knew this was not normal, but didn't know how to make the thoughts go away. She read her Bible, attended church, and prayed, but it all felt meaningless.

Two years previously in her senior year of college, Carla admitted that she had suffered a bout of depression that lasted a month. The previous episode wasn't quite as severe, and it resolved on its own. At this point, Carla was losing weight, and her energy level was low. After completing a history and physical exam and ordering some laboratory tests to rule out other physical disorders, I diagnosed Carla with major depressive disorder (MDD). I referred Carla for counseling and also started her on a type of antidepressant called a selective serotonin reuptake inhibitor. We also talked about incorporating nutrition, exercise, and a healthy lifestyle. I saw Carla for follow-up four weeks later, and her depression had markedly improved. She was no longer troubled with thoughts of dying and she felt closer to God.

Carla's story is a classic story for MDD. She fits the most common age group and gender, and she had a prior bout of depression, which put her at increased risk of recurrence. Because of the severity of her depression, a combination of medication and counseling was the recommended treatment. I encouraged Carla to continue to pursue prayer and meditation. This became easier for her to do as her brain came into better physical balance. I advised Carla to stay on the medication for a minimum of one year. Many patients stop their medication after a few months because they feel better and then end up spiraling back into depression. Unfortunately, the depression often recurs within six months. The goal of treatment with medication is to help establish healthy chemical pathways in the brain. For these pathways to become strong, they need to be used extensively, which takes time. When the medications are stopped early, the brain tends to revert to the older, more established negative pathways. Research shows that people who have had one bout of major depression have a 50 percent chance of recurrence in their lifetime, and that rate goes up by about 16 percent with each recurrence. Depression is unhealthy for the brain, so treatment is aimed at avoiding recurrence.

There are many causative factors that play into mood disorders—physical, psychological, and spiritual. We are body, mind, and spirit, all of which are interconnected and interdependent. Illness in one area can quickly affect the other areas. Our brain is an amazing organ, but a physical organ nonetheless. It can become injured or become deficient in proper neurotransmitter (brain chemistry) balance to the extent that it does not work properly and mood is affected. For such patients, medications may be quite helpful in restoring the proper balance of neurotransmitters.

Throughout this book, I am going to liken neural pathways in the brain either to the branching structures of trees or pathways. If you are interested in more information on this subject, I recommend *Who Switched Off My Brain?*[3] by Caroline Leaf.

Our brain is an incredibly complex structure and is comprised of individual cells called neurons. These neurons have tendrils called dendrites that reach out and connect with other brain cells via an electrochemical pathway or synapse. If neurons connect frequently, the pathways become strong, interconnected, and entrenched.

My husband and I like to go camping (glamping to be exact) in the Northern California redwoods. Due to the extreme moisture, there is a lot of plant growth in the forest. We recently walked on a trail that had not been used for some time. It was overgrown and difficult to navigate. Our progress was unusually slow, and we got lost a bit as we tried to find the trail again. We later came to a path that was frequently used. It was wide and easy to navigate, and we made fast progress on this part of the trail. Your thought patterns are like these pathways. If you tend to dwell frequently on what is good or positive in your life, these pathways will become dominant, and your thoughts will naturally travel down these paths even at rest. Alternatively, if you tend to think about yourself negatively, worry, feel angry, or have other toxic thought patterns, this too will become a dominant pathway in your brain. Dwelling in these negative pathways will make it difficult to access feelings of peace and joy. The point here is that your brain will naturally use the wider, well-traveled pathway. The goal of treatment is to develop a widely used pathway that takes you to peace and joy quickly.

Every pathway your thoughts travel has a corresponding chemical response. Each and every thought you have releases chemicals, some of which can be healthy and others harmful. When you set your mind on things that are true, noble, right, admirable, lovely, etc. (see Phil. 4:8), dopamine, serotonin, endorphins, and numerous other positive neurotransmitters are released from your brain that promote health in your body. Conversely, worry, fear, anger, bitterness, hatred, envy, and other negative emotions cause the release of chemicals that break up the healthy pathways in your brain and promote disease.

Good thoughts release chemicals that create healthy neural networks.

Negative thoughts release chemicals that break up healthy neural networks.

TREES OF YOUR MIND

This point may be obvious, but I want to emphasize that your emotions or feelings are not separate from your thought processes. Think of your feelings as the fruit that grows from a particular thought tree. We all know that you cannot get cherries from a lemon tree. The fruit tells you exactly what type of tree is growing. In fact, Paul describes love, joy, peace, patience, kindness, goodness, faithfulness, gentleness, and self-control as the fruit of the Spirit (see Gal. 5:22-23). To reap this type of fruit, your tree must be deeply rooted in the understanding of the finished work of the cross. I will call this tree the Tree of Faith. The more I meditate on what Christ has done for me and the spiritual blessings and promises I have in Him, the stronger my branches (neural pathways) become. Soon I begin to experience the feelings (fruit) of joy, peace, kindness, and so forth generated from these neural pathways. These feelings are the natural outcome of thought patterns rooted deep in my core beliefs about my identity in Christ and who Christ is in me. I believe that nothing can separate me from His love and that all of His promises are true. How then can I lose? What weapon formed against me will prosper?

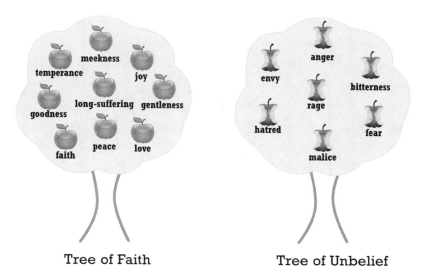

Tree of Faith   Tree of Unbelief

TREE OF FAITH VERSUS TREE OF UNBELIEF

How big your Tree of Faith becomes is dependent on how big you allow another tree to grow in the garden of your mind. I will call this poisonous tree the Tree of Unbelief. Unbelief is rampant among believers, and from it other sins are generated. This tree is rooted in double-minded thoughts, unsure whether God is always good, doubting the faithfulness of God, always wondering whether or not God may be waiting to punish, or perhaps does not love you as much as He loves others. This Tree of Unbelief produces fruit as well. This is the poisonous fruit of anxiety, fear, depression, anger, jealousy, envy, etc. Such "fruit" is toxic to the Tree of Faith. The chemicals released by these emotions interrupt the pathways that develop the Tree of Faith and prohibit the fruit of joy and peace from developing. These two trees do not grow well together, and one will always dominate the other.

There is another poisonous tree that can grow in the garden of your mind, and this is the Tree of Offense. This tree is rooted in the soil of unforgiveness, and it produces the fruit of bitterness and hatred, which can lead to anxiety and depression. This particular tree is quite dangerous, poisoning the soil of your mind, making it impossible to grow a healthy Tree of Faith. I liken it to cancer, spreading and contaminating all of your thought processes. We will talk more about unforgiveness in another chapter.

Tree of Unbelief   Tree of Offense   Tree of Faith
(Rooted from a seed of unforgiveness)

In summary, anxiety and depression affect millions of people, and there are different types of anxiety and depressive disorders. It is important to remember that feelings of anxiety and depression are the *fruit* of the *trees* that grow in our thought life. Although we cannot take our feelings captive, we are commanded to take every thought captive to the obedience of Christ.

There are three major thought trees that grow in our mind—the Tree of Faith, the Tree of Unbelief, and the Tree of Offense. If we nourish the Tree of Faith, our thoughts will produce positive feelings like joy and peace. However, if the Tree of Unbelief or the Tree of Offense is dominant in our thought life, negative feelings like worry, fear, sadness, jealousy, anger, and bitterness will be produced.

ACTION POINTS

1.   What are my most common feelings?

_____

_____

_____

_____

_____

2.   What are the thoughts and imaginations I have that are not captive to the obedience of Christ?

_____

_____

_____

_____

3.   What are the results (actions or inactions) that result from my feelings?

_____
_____
_____
_____
_____

4. What are the thoughts that produce my feelings (if my feelings are the fruit, then what is the tree that produces the fruit)?

_____
_____
_____
_____

5. Which tree is dominant in my mind (the Tree of Faith or Unbelief)?

_____
_____
_____
_____

6. Is the Tree of Offense growing in my thoughts? If so, why?

_____
_____
_____
_____

7. Spend some time in prayer and ask God to show you any areas of unbelief and offense. As you find them, repent and ask the Father to

forgive you and fill you with faith. This is an exercise we do repeatedly throughout our life.

NOTES

1. *Diagnostic and Statistical Manual of Mental Disorders: DSM-IV-TR*, 4th ed. (Washington, DC: American Psychiatric Association, 2000).

2. "NIH Fact Sheets: Mood Disorders," U.S. National Library of Medicine, March 29, 2013, http://report.nih.gov/NIHfactsheets/ViewFactSheet. aspx?csid=48.

3. Caroline Leaf, *Who Switched off My Brain? Controlling Toxic Thoughts and Emotions* (Nashville, TN: Thomas Nelson Publishers, 2009).

Chapter 3

What Is the Root?

*"Happiness is not a goal...it's a
byproduct of a life well lived."*
—ELEANOR ROOSEVELT

WHAT IS THE ROOT OF ANXIETY AND DEPRESSION?

It is my belief that we are created with a body (physical), mind (psychological or soul), and spirit. Although these three entities are distinct, they are interconnected. Dysfunction in one area can quickly affect the other two areas. So much so that it becomes difficult to pull them apart or to treat them separately. When I evaluate a patient, one of the first things I do is find out where the root of the mood disorder lies. Does this patient have a physical problem, such as an endocrine dysfunction, which may be causing their anxiety? Or perhaps the root is psychological due to their fear of failure or feelings of worthlessness. Maybe the cause is spiritual. I have discovered that patients who struggle with unforgiveness, anger, pornography, lying, stealing, etc. often have depression because sin affects the spirit man. If I can't identify the root, I will end up treating recurring symptoms and the patient will not get better. Frequently, I end up treating all three areas because most patients have had their anxiety or depression for some time, and all three realms are affected.

PHYSICAL CAUSES OF ANXIETY AND DEPRESSION

Some people don't understand that the brain is a physical organ and subject to injury. We can't just tell people to pray more or to stop worrying and be happy. The brain requires adequate oxygen, nutrition, and a complex balance of hormones and neurotransmitter chemicals to function properly. Any condition that upsets this balance can cause anxiety and depression. Some common examples include thyroid and hormonal disorders, each of which can easily be found by a simple blood test. The thyroid gland regulates many other endocrine and hormone functions in the body. When the thyroid does not work properly, many other systems suffer. If you have a mood disorder, make sure that your medical provider has checked your thyroid.

Hormonal dysfunction for women, particularly during perimenopause, is a common physical cause for anxiety and depression. Cheryl, 44 years of age, came into my office in tears convinced that she was losing her mind. She had two children, the youngest being two years old, and she had not had a period in the last three months. She was waking up at night with frequent hot flashes, which caused sleep deprivation. She felt irritable and depressed, which was unusual for her. As this woman sat in my office, she repeated her story several times, a classic symptom of anxiety. When I took her history, it became apparent that her onset of symptoms was quite rapid and related to the cessation of her menses. She had no prior history of anxiety or mood disorder. The root cause for the mood disorder was physical and directly related to the drop in her estrogen due to menopause and sleep deprivation. Estrogen can have a profound effect on serotonin, which is why women can be irritable the week prior to their menses as estrogen levels drop. During menopause, the ovaries begin to produce less estrogen and some women are acutely sensitive to this change and suffer profound mood disorder. I treated Cheryl with hormone replacement, and when I saw her for the follow-up next month, her mood had completely normalized. Hormone replacement has both risks and benefits and is not necessarily a treatment I recommend for every woman. Treatment must be individualized to the needs, concerns, risks, and benefits of each patient. Women who have had breast cancer or who are at risk for blood clots, heart attack, or stroke should not take hormone replacement therapy. On the other hand, hormone replacement can have a profound benefit for some women.

Testosterone deficiency in men can cause fatigue, low libido, and mood disorder, particularly depression. Often treating the underlying deficiency can improve mood tremendously. A simple blood test can determine if the testosterone level is within the normal range. Men who are over the age of 50 and are taking testosterone supplementation should make sure they get an annual PSA blood test to monitor for prostate cancer. Testosterone can cause prostate cancer to accelerate, and men who have had prostate cancer should not take testosterone.

Another common physical cause of depression is chronic pain. I have numerous patients in my practice with debilitating neck or back pain or disorders such as rheumatoid arthritis or fibromyalgia. These patients hurt all of the time, and their pain limits what they can do. The constant stress of pain and limitation in daily activities causes depletion of neurotransmitters in the brain. Other types of chronic conditions linked to depression include heart disease and emphysema. Patients who have had a brain injury or who have dementia often undergo changes in personality or mood as areas of their brain no longer function properly. I have seen patients who were normally happy and stable in their mood develop profound anxiety and fear as dementia affected the chemical balance of the brain.

Sleep deprivation is another physical cause of anxiety and depression. Neurotransmitters are replenished during the rapid eye movement (REM) cycle of sleep. When REM sleep is inadequate, people can become anxious and depressed because of depleted neurotransmitters. People who are at risk for sleep deprivation are those with insomnia and those working rotating schedules or night shifts. Another category of risk is those who are caring for infants, toddlers, and special needs. Women in perimenopause, those traveling in multiple time zone changes, and those keeping a hectic schedule with too little downtime are also at risk for sleep deprivation. Another major risk factor for inadequate REM sleep is sleep apnea, a condition in which people stop breathing during sleep. As the oxygen level drops in your bloodstream due to a blocked airway, the brain signals your body to wake up and move to reposition your airway. People with sleep apnea don't get quality REM sleep. This condition is very stressful to the brain and results in a release of cortisol, which has negative effects on the brain and vascular system, increasing the risk for hypertension and heart disease. If you snore, are overweight, or have restless legs and don't feel refreshed when you awaken in the morning ask your medical provider to order a sleep study. Sleep apnea is considered a significant risk factor for resistant depression.

Alcohol and drugs have a profound effect on neurotransmitters and can cause substantial anxiety and depression. Unless the patient is willing to stop the substance abuse, their mood disorder cannot be successfully treated. That being said, people often self-medicate with alcohol and drugs because of an underlying mood disorder. Once the substance abuse is removed, the anxiety and depression can become quite apparent. If the underlying psychiatric condition is not treated, the patient is at high risk for recurrence of the substance abuse.

Anna, a 22-year-old woman, came in to see me because of uncontrollable anxiety. During the exam, I noticed that her blood pressure was quite high. I asked her about alcohol usage, and she admitted to drinking up to ten servings of alcohol daily. She didn't think it was a problem but agreed with me that she should stop. Over the next year, she went into an alcohol recovery program twice. During recovery, her blood pressure and anxiety would improve, but then she would go back to drinking and her symptoms would recur. Medication was ineffective in treating this patient, and until she decided to stop the alcohol, there wasn't much I could do medically for her.

There also seems to be a hereditary component to some anxiety and depressive disorders. Some people are genetically more vulnerable to anxiety and depression and may have defective neurotransmitter pathways. I have several of these patients in my practice. These people have a history of anxiety and depression that goes back to childhood and often have several family members who suffer from mood disorders. Medication can be quite helpful for these people as counseling alone is not always effective.

The physical causes above are not meant to be an exhaustive list. There can be other physical causes for anxiety and depression as well. Make sure that you or your loved one has a thorough physical exam and some laboratory tests to rule out a physical cause for anxiety or depression.

When the root is physical, medication is often the treatment of choice if the underlying condition cannot be adequately resolved. Counseling is not going to fix injured or dysfunctional brain chemistry.

SHOULD MEDICATION BE USED TO TREAT ANXIETY AND DEPRESSION?

"Should I take medication?" This is a question I get asked frequently. People have misperceptions and often feel guilty about taking medication for anxiety and depression. Christians in particular struggle with shame when medication is recommended. Medications can be very useful, but they need to be used in the correct context and are not without potential side effects. Common misperceptions about medication include concerns about dependency, long-term or permanent side effects, and perceptions that the risk of side effects is worse than the mood disorder. Sometimes people think that using a medication is "cheating" and won't allow you to get to the root of the problem. What they don't realize is that the root may be physical and that medications can restore a normal chemical balance in the brain so that counseling can be effective.

The vast majority of medications that are used for the treatment of anxiety and depression do not cause dependency or addiction. The exceptions are benzodiazepines (Valium, Xanax, Ativan, Klonopin, etc.), which do not have indications for long-term anxiety treatment. This class of drugs should be used cautiously due to dependency, withdrawal side effects, and increased risk of developing dementia with long-term use.

Medications that are safe to use long term include fluoxetine, paroxetine, sertraline, citalopram, escitalopram, venlafaxine, bupropion, duloxetine, etc. These medications can improve function in the serotonin, dopamine, and norepinephrine pathways of the brain. Common side effects include drowsiness or insomnia, sweating, dry mouth, nausea, and changes in libido. Most of these side effects are short term and resolve as your body adjusts to the change in neurotransmitters brought about by these medications. If the side effects are not tolerable, your medical provider can either stop the medication or try another. I usually advise a minimum treatment length of 12 months. Shorter treatment times have higher failure rates. The purpose of using medication is to restore normal neurotransmitter balance and to create healthy pathways that are strong. This process takes time. The problem is that patients often feel great after a few months and think they no longer need their medication. They stop the medication and after a month or two end up right back where they started. Their pathways had not been normalized for a long enough period of time to be maintained.

If the patient is stable after a year of treatment and they are not in a period of increased stress, I look at a trial of tapering the patient off the medication. Most medications need to be tapered for a few weeks to reduce side effects. If the patient is stable in their mood, I leave them off, and if not, I restart. Some people are successful in getting off of medication, but others truly need long term medication. Obviously, medication is an adjunct treatment. That means that patients also need to incorporate diet, exercise, sleep, counseling, prayer, meditation, etc. For some, this is not enough, and medication is what brings about normalcy and balance to the brain.

Medications are indicated for moderate to severe depression and anxiety. On one hand, I see patients who want medication when what they need to do is to change their lifestyle and get some counseling and prayer. And on the other, I see patients who have profound, prolonged anxiety/depression who have done everything they know to do. These patients are eating healthy, exercising, pursuing counseling, seeking God in prayer, and repenting of anything and everything. But no matter what they do, they can't get out of the spiral of despair or anxiety. These are the patients to whom I recommend adjunct treatment with medication. I will also recommend medication when a patient has a physical component such as family history of depression or anxiety, chronic pain, emphysema, heart disease, etc.

I want to reiterate the fact that the brain is a physical organ, and sometimes suffers neurotransmitter dysfunction that can be substantially improved with medication. If someone had diabetes, we would never tell them just to think or pray their glucose into control because we understand that their pancreas is damaged and no longer makes insulin as it should. We would not criticize someone who took medication to normalize their blood sugar (as long as they were making appropriate lifestyle changes as well). Unfortunately the same cannot be said for antidepressant medication. Sadly, I hear the all too frequent stories of people being chastised by their friends and family for taking medication when it's truly indicated.

Medications are not a panacea, neither are they to be despised. They are a very useful tool, derived from the study of the human brain and are a blessing from God when used correctly. For many, medications bring the healing needed to restore normal brain function. We do a tremendous disservice to those suffering from anxiety and depression when we deny them this benefit out of misunderstanding or ignorance.

PSYCHOLOGICAL CAUSES OF ANXIETY AND DEPRESSION

Psychological causes of anxiety and depression are related to thinking patterns and what we believe to be true about our self, others, and God. These thought patterns go back to very early childhood and can be heavily influenced by how we were raised. Were the adults in our life trustworthy, reliable, and loving, or were they cruel, abusive, distant, or just plain absent? Perhaps we struggled in school, which made us feel stupid, or perhaps we felt unattractive. Children perceive feelings as truth, and these early thought patterns can become entrenched even when we "know" they aren't true as we become adults. What I have described above are internal pressures, and they are a very limited sampling of potential causes of anxiety and depression.

Other internal pressures can come from our culture. Every culture applies pressures or expectations that affect our thought processes. For example, our culture tells men they must be strong and productive and that they cannot show weakness. For women, the expectation is they must be beautiful, the perfect wife and mother, and have a successful career. We are exposed to these cultural expectations from infancy and our perceived inability to meet these standards can often result in anxiety or depression.

There can be external pressures that affect mood as well. Paul describes his trip to Macedonia as "conflicts on the outside, fears within" (2 Cor. 7:5). When there has been a loss, or particularly a series of losses, people can become depressed. It is not uncommon for me to see people in the office who are suffering profound emotional pain after a break in a significant relationship, loss of a job, the death of a loved one, or bankruptcy. Sometimes these losses can cause severe anxiety and depression, so much so that the person cannot function at home or work. The stresses become more difficult to manage when they are prolonged; such as a bad marriage, unhappy workplace, adult children with substance abuse problems, or trying to work and care for elderly family members. These are obviously just a few of the many stresses that can affect our thinking patterns and our feelings. Anything that we feel powerless to change can affect our mood.

Counseling can be very helpful for people to identify and change thinking patterns. Cognitive behavioral therapy in particular is very useful for the treatment of anxiety and depression. This type of therapy helps people identify the thoughts and feelings behind their actions. Therapists will often provide tools for patients to use when they feel acutely anxious or depressed. I have seen more success treating my patients with anxiety and depression when they are actively seeking counseling. Medications can change brain chemistry, but they don't change underlying thought processes or lies you believe about yourself or God.

I believe that the root of most, if not all of the psychological causes of anxiety and depression is a lack of understanding and/or belief in the goodness of God, how much God loves us, and our identity in Christ. If we really understood and believed that we are beloved beyond time and measure and that we are currently seated with Christ in heavenly realms as described by Paul in Ephesians, there would be nothing that could cause prolonged discouragement.

I do not want to minimize grieving over a loss. Grieving in a healthy manner is necessary for our mental health, and for some people this takes longer than others. Jesus Himself wept when He heard the news that Lazarus had died. There is a time for grieving, but joy comes in the morning. God walks us *through* the valley of the shadow of death. We are not supposed to stay in the valley forever. Some people get stuck in the valley and live there as a lifestyle. If you are trapped in the valley, chances are good that you believe a lie. Find a counselor who will help you identify the lie and get you moving out of the valley.

SPIRITUAL CAUSES OF ANXIETY AND DEPRESSION

We are not alone. There are demonic forces that can come against us, which directly affect our mood. Kris Vallotton wrote *Spirit Wars*, in which he describes evil spirits that can come against us with oppression, fear, unbelief, and suicidality, to name a few. It is my belief that there are two main reasons God allows evil forces to have access into our lives. The first is because of sin and the second is to train us to be conquerors. God allows Satan a certain amount of activity for His purposes, but it's not meant to punish us or to be a permanent condition. There is no contest between God and Satan. They are not equivalents of good and evil or light and dark. God is far superior to Satan, and there are two angels to every demon. Satan is limited, and God is not. God is omnipresent; Satan is not. It's not an equal contest, and the end result is known. We win.

Sin itself opens us up to demonic activity as it gives evil forces access to taunt us and make us feel guilty and unclean. This is the reason Paul said not to sin in your anger, lest you give the enemy a "foothold" (Eph. 4:26-27).

I had seen William several times in the office for numerous symptoms, and I finally diagnosed him with major depressive disorder. He admitted to great feelings of guilt and unworthiness that he couldn't seem to shake. As I dug a bit, I found that although this man was a believer in Christ, he struggled with pornography. The pornography was causing great stress in his marriage, and he felt distant from God. Obviously, there were psychological forces at play that triggered a perceived "need" for pornography, but his inability to stop the sin had opened him to tremendous torment from demonic forces. Until he truly repented and got to the root of his feelings of inadequacy that caused him to desire pornography, this man would not get better. Although medication might alleviate some of his symptoms, it would never treat the underlying root.

A good example of this principle is the life of King Saul. When David returned from a victorious battle, the women sang, "Saul has slain his thousands, and David his ten thousands" (1 Sam. 18:7 NKJV). Saul became jealous and angry, and God sent a "distressing" spirit that came upon him. This evil spirit tormented and oppressed Saul for the rest of his life. Saul not only became fearful and anxious but began to have delusional thoughts and psychotic rages. In other words, the sin of jealousy exposed Saul to demonic forces that caused Saul to believe lies that permanently affected his mood. If Saul had repented, the evil spirit would have departed, and Saul would have been able to think correctly.

Other times demonic forces can come against us, just as they did to Job. Job was righteous, yet God allowed demonic forces to come and test him through tremendous financial loss, the death of his family, and his health. These losses caused Job tremendous emotional pain, so much so that he cursed the day of his birth (see Job 3:1).

When we sin, God allows demonic forces to oppress us as a means to get our attention with the goal of repentance. Although we may not perceive it as such, this is His mercy at work on our behalf. He also allows us to be tested by demonic forces so we can become strong. His intent is always our victory. And to that end, He has given us armor and weaponry, which is discussed in another chapter.

THE SIN OF UNBELIEF

As mentioned in the previous chapter, unbelief causes us to be double-minded, and there is no peace in double-mindedness.

You will keep in perfect peace those whose minds are steadfast, because they trust in you (Isaiah 26:3).

Although any sin opens us up to demonic activity, the sin of unbelief is particularly powerful. So much so, I am going to speak to it specifically. I believe that unbelief is the primary root of fear and that fear is what causes most anxiety. Unbelief is the most socially acceptable sin in the church today. If we knew that fellow church members were dabbling in pornography, shoplifting, slander, or other obvious sin patterns we'd probably talk to them about their behavior and expect consequences. However, we often accept the unbelief of others and even offer our sympathies. We don't treat unbelief like Jesus did.

Jesus was extremely interested in faith. He was moved by the faith of people, not their desperation. When the Gentile woman from Canaan pleaded with Him to heal her demon-possessed daughter, He initially declined. This was a desperate woman. Jesus must have offended her when He compared her to a dog, not worthy of the children's bread. Yet her response was one of such faith that Jesus changed His mind, healed her daughter, and commented on her great faith. Did you know that your faith has the potential to change God's mind?

Jesus was very disappointed when He did not find faith. Unbelief limited His ability to perform the miraculous (see Matt. 13:58), and he was distressed with the disciples for their unbelief on several occasions. So much so that He rebuked them when they did not believe the reports of His resurrection (see Mark 16:14).

There are numerous lies that we believe that can cause our unbelief. Identifying these lies is an important key to freedom, which is discussed in a later chapter.

Faith is a big deal to God. We cannot please Him apart from faith and when He returns, He is wondering if He will find it in you.

> *However, when the Son of Man comes, will he find faith on the earth?* (Luke 18:8)

In summary, we were created with a body, mind, and spirit. Anxiety and depression can be rooted in the body, mind, or spirit but quickly affect the other areas as well. Treatment must be geared toward treating the root or the mood disorder will not improve. Although lifestyle, counseling, and prayer are appropriate treatments to use for the treatment of anxiety and depression, medications may also be necessary and appropriate.

ACTION POINTS

1. If you have had anxiety of depression for many years and have other chronic medical conditions or a family history of mood disorders, you may have a physical root. If you cannot determine an obvious cause for your anxiety or depression, make sure that you have discussed your condition with your medical provider and have been checked for any underlying medical conditions.

2. Are you getting at least eight hours of sleep per night? If you struggle with insomnia or have any of the risk factors for sleep apnea discussed above, talk to your medical provider about getting a sleep study.

3. Have you been made to feel guilty by yourself or others for using medication to treat your anxiety or depression? If you have been to counseling and have tried the nonpharmaceutical tools described in this book without improvement, there is a good chance your mood disorder has a physical root. Realize that the guilt is rooted in a lie and be grateful that there are medications available to help you, just as there are for other chronic physical conditions.

4. Can you identify any internal or external pressures that contribute to your anxiety or depression? If so, what are they and what do you think God would say about them?

_____

_____

_____

_____

_____

5. Can you identify any chronic sin patterns that have opened you up to oppression (unforgiveness, lying, stealing, gossip, sexual sin, etc.)? If so, what do you need to repent of?

_____

_____

_____

_____

_____

6. Do you struggle with unbelief? If so, in what areas?

_____

_____

_____

----

7.   Unbelief is connected to lies that we believe about our self, others, or God. As you read through the following chapters, dig to find the root lies. Repenting of unbelief and replacing these lies with truth is how you get freedom from unbelief.

Chapter 4

Identify the Lie

"What people believe prevails over the truth."
—SOPHOCLES

I n this next set of chapters, psychological aspects or thinking patterns that affect our mood will be outlined. Many of these thinking patterns are ingrained from our early years and have become habitual. The process of how we think can be changed with a bit of work and is the basis of cognitive behavioral therapy (CBT).

You can control your thoughts and take them captive, and in fact you are the only one who can do so. Think of it as clearing a new trail that's overgrown with brush. The more you clear and travel the trail, the quicker you go. When you read through these next few chapters and discover a personal negative thought pattern, I want you to imagine yourself putting up a Hazard, No Trespassing sign. These are thought paths you will not give yourself permission to travel any longer. They are now out of bounds or forbidden to you. Instead, grasp on to the positive patterns described in these chapters and visualize yourself putting up a large Welcome to Joy and Enter Here sign with green lights. These are the new thought patterns that your brain will travel and eventually own.

A word of caution here. These new patterns will *feel* unfamiliar and uncomfortable or perhaps "too good to be true." This is expected when you enter new territory. When you travel into a new town, it doesn't feel familiar or comfortable. However, if you've been to that town a few times, you quickly feel right at home. This same principle applies to thought patterns. The more frequently you travel these pathways, the more real they will *feel* to you.

Tearing down lies often creates a domino effect. Once you pull down a lie, a whole new area of thinking that was previously inaccessible opens up to you. Some lies are more powerful than others. If you can take down a big foundational lie, a bunch of other lies are often removed at the same time. On the other hand, if you pick around the edges at the smaller lies without changing the foundational lie, freedom remains elusive.

The ancient quote by Sophocles above is powerful and holds true today. What I believe about myself, others, or God, whether true or not, remains "true" to me and I will think, speak, and act out of what I perceive to be true.

> The greatest deception men suffer is from their own opinions.
> —Leonardo da Vinci

Our belief systems are strongholds, and they affect how we perceive the world around us. These strongholds are powerful places of dominion that control our thoughts, speech, and actions. If these strongholds are under the lordship of Christ, then our thoughts, words, and actions in that area will reflect the attributes of Christ.

For example, if I *believe* that God is always good, I will *think* that God wants the best for me. I will *speak* statements that declare His goodness in every area of my life because I expect His goodness. I will *act* in faith and confidence, knowing that I am under His protection. Conversely, if I *believe* that God is fickle or just waiting to punish me when I err, I will *think* that God is unpredictable and not to be trusted. I will *speak* statements that reflect my lack of faith, and I will *act* by limiting what I do to what I perceive to be safe.

People with each of these outlooks will perceive the same set of facts quite differently. Let's say I've just received a termination notice from my employer, and I don't have another job waiting in the wings. Fortunately, I believe what Paul wrote about God:

> *"What no eye has seen, what no ear has heard, and what no human mind has conceived"*—*the things God has prepared for those who love him* (1 Corinthians 2:9).

Because I believe that God is always good, I am confident that He will provide for me and I will lack nothing. I think God has good things for me, so He must have allowed me to be terminated because He has something better for me. I look at this situation as a positive opportunity. However, if the stronghold in my mind is that God is not fully trustworthy, I will view this change with dread. I will be afraid that there will not be enough money to pay my bills and that my next job (assuming I get another job) won't be as desirable as the one I've just lost. Even though I've read the same Scripture above, I don't believe it's true for me in my current situation, so it holds little value for me.

Anna is 26 now and has been my patient for several years. When Anna was 16, her mother brought her in to see me because she was concerned about her daughter's weight and poor eating habits. This young girl was 67 inches tall and only weighed 105 pounds. Her body mass index put her solidly in the underweight category. Anna told me she thought her eating habits were fine and that she ate "plenty." When I expressed concern, Anna disagreed that she was underweight. Her mother told me that Anna frequently made comments about how fat she was and that she skipped breakfast and lunch. When we defined what Anna meant by "plenty," it was obviously inadequate.

You may know people like Anna. This young girl believed herself to be fat, regardless of what the scale read. When I looked at Anna, I saw a very lovely, malnourished girl whose clothing hung shapelessly on her thin frame. Yet Anna saw an ugly, fat girl when she looked in the mirror. Anna's belief about herself was stronger than the truth. I could repeatedly tell Anna that she was severely underweight, and even though it was true Anna could not perceive this to be so. I referred Anna to counseling, which revealed a deeper lie that drove her behavior. Anna believed herself to be unlovable.

I will reiterate another point that I made in an earlier chapter, and that is, we must have congruence between what we know in our minds and what we believe in our hearts. An elderly patient of mine, a man who has been a sincere follower of Christ for more than 60 years, can quote the entire chapter of Psalm 91. In spite of this, he struggles with anxiety because his soul does not believe what the Word says. He is an unbelieving believer, an unfortunately common condition.

Knowing and believing must be in agreement for a truth to be felt.

So what is the truth? I will put it simply. To know God is to know the truth. God is the complete truth, and there is no deceit or shadow of turning in Him. Jesus Himself said:

I am the way and the truth and the life (John 14:6).

We must fully grasp that God is truth and that everything He states is true—not just partially or sometimes true, but always and completely true.

All your words are true; all your righteous laws are eternal (Psalm 119:160).

The elderly gentleman I described above is double-minded. There is no peace for him in double-mindedness because he is torn between two masters.

God wants us to know Him, and in knowing Him grace and peace are found in abundance.

Grace and peace be yours in abundance through the knowledge of God and of Jesus our Lord (2 Peter 1:2).

Peter then goes on to say that through our knowledge of Him we have everything we need for a godly life so that we may participate in His divine nature (see 2 Peter 1:3-4). Did you get that? Through *knowing* Him, we are given the ability to participate in the very nature of God. God's nature is not one of depression, anxiety, or fear but of love, hope, peace, and joy. We have access to this nature by knowing Him.

So how do you *know* God? To get to know someone, you have to spend time with them, read what they've written, and listen to what they've said. When I fell in love with my husband, I wanted to know everything about him. I asked all sorts of questions to find out how he thought and to understand his background and character. I spent hours on the phone with him and took every opportunity to be with him. I wanted to not only know the big things, like his family background, but I wanted to know the little things, such as his favorite foods and favorite color. I wanted to *know* him. It is the same way with God. To know God, I must read what He's written, listen to what He says, and spend time with Him.

The written Word of God is invaluable in describing God's character. The word of God is living and active, and it changes how we think. The word of God washes our minds by bringing us into truth and changing how we think.

The fear of the Lord is the beginning of wisdom, and knowledge of the Holy One is understanding (Proverbs 9:10).

Spend time reading and meditating on what God has written. It's not enough to be able to memorize the truth. You have to meditate and allow the truth to penetrate not just your intellect but your soul. You may need to spend days or weeks on one passage of Scripture to grasp the truth, and that's okay. Stay there until the truth transforms your heart and mind, until you actually *feel* the truth and it is real to you. Remember, unless something feels true to you, it will just be a theory.

I have not departed from the commands of his lips; I have treasured the words of his mouth more than my daily bread (Job 23:12).

I want to make an additional point, and that is that the purpose of the Word is to bring you into an encounter with God. There are many people who know Scriptures, including Satan himself. Knowing Scripture doesn't mean you *know* God. For example, I could tell you a variety of facts about Abraham Lincoln because there is much written about him. I could list where he was born, whom he married, and even what he said. But I don't *know* Abraham Lincoln. Can you imagine just reading letters someone had written but never actually meeting them? How would you really know them, unless you talked to them? That is how it is with God. The purpose of the Word is to draw us into a relationship. In addition, it is the Holy Spirit, a living person, who unveils the mystery of the Word as we read it. The Word of God is layered and deep, much of it is hidden to those who don't believe. As you read the Word, ask the Holy Spirit to reveal the strongholds in your mind that are not under the lordship of Christ. Allow the water of the Word to wash away the lies.

When your words came, I ate them; they were my joy and my heart's delight, for I bear your name, Lord God Almighty (Jeremiah 15:16).

We all struggle with lies at some level because satan, the father of lies, is active in this present age. When we agree with the lies that satan tells us, we cede to him authority in that particular stronghold of our minds. Until the lie is exchanged for truth, we will struggle in that area. Knowing God is what protects us from lies. When we do not know Him well, we are unable to discern truth, and we end up relying on what *feels* real to us. Here are some of the most prevalent lies that keep us stuck.

I am not completely forgiven. Therefore, I deserve to be punished (Lie).

If you frequently feel a consistent, underlying shame, then you believe this lie. Although we may theoretically believe that our sins are forgiven, many of us feel a lingering guilt for what we've done. This shame makes us *feel* we should be punished. The truth is that we are completely forgiven, and God does not punish His children. Jesus paid for *all* of our sins on the cross. If you believe this lie, then you think the cross was inadequate, and that through a penance you can make up for what the cross can't cover. The truth is that we cannot possibly earn forgiveness; it is a gift to us from Jesus.

If we confess our sins, he is faithful and just and will forgive us our sins and purify us from all unrighteousness (1 John 1:9).

The companion lie to this is:

I am a sinner saved by grace (Lie).

I suspect there are alarm bells going off in your head as you read this, but there is a subtle lie in this statement that completely distorts how we view ourselves. I did not grow up believing that I was a saint. I was taught that I was just a sinner saved by grace. It is true that I *was* a sinner saved by grace. However, I was given a new nature in baptism. Paul writes:

> *We are those who have died to sin; how can we live in it any longer? Or don't you know that all of us who were baptized into Christ Jesus were baptized into his death? We were therefore buried with him through baptism into death in order that, just as Christ was raised from the dead through the glory of the Father, we too may live a new life* (Romans 6:2-4).

My old man, the old nature that desired sinful things, died. Or at least it was supposed to! I think some of us need to go back to baptism and hold the old man under a little longer! This old nature *should* no longer rule us. Does it still? I suspect all of us would say yes in at least some area of our lives. If you are struggling with sin, this is indicative of strongholds in your mind that are not under the lordship of Jesus. Paul says:

> *For we know that our old self was crucified with him so that the body of sin might be done away with, that we should no longer be slaves to sin* (Romans 6:6).

We have no excuses. There should be no contest between our old man and the spirit of Christ that lives in us. The famous saying, "The devil made me do it," has no place in the life of a follower of Jesus. We were given the ability to live a life free from sin to the extent that we choose to do so. I am not stating we are sinless after salvation. There is only One who is sinless. But we are called to be holy as He is holy. God would not command us to something if He did not give us the grace to do so. He actually expects us to live holy lives. This is why Paul could say, *"count yourselves dead to sin but alive to God in Christ Jesus,"* and *"sin shall no longer be your master, because you are not under the law, but under grace"* (Rom. 6:11,14).

Grace is not a permission to excuse sin but a supernatural provision to live a life free from sin. This is why Paul says:

> *You have been set free from sin and have become slaves to righteousness* (Romans 6:18).

Think about that for a moment. Have you been set free from sin? Are you a slave to righteousness? Is that true for you? I will admit it's a process for me. When I realized that God saw me as holy because of Christ, it changed how I viewed myself. I now expect myself not to sin because I know the spirit of Christ lives in me and has given me the grace to choose holiness in every situation. Do I sin? I do, but it's less than previously, and I am quite grieved when I do so. When I viewed myself as "just a sinner, saved by grace," I was not surprised when I messed up. After all, that's what sinners do. I figured that was just my nature, and God would need to forgive me again.

> *But you are not controlled by your sinful nature. You are controlled by the Spirit if you have the Spirit of God living in you* (Romans 8:9 NLT).

It is interesting to note that when Paul wrote to the Romans he addressed them as saints: *"To all who are in Rome, beloved of God, called to be saints"* (Rom. 1:7 NKJV). He didn't write to them as sinners because their identity had changed to one of holiness.

> *Therefore, if anyone is in Christ, the new creation has come: The old has gone, the new is here!* (2 Corinthians 5:17)

So why do we sin? We sin because there are areas in our mind that need to be renewed, areas controlled by lies. Why would you gossip about another if you truly believed it hurt the other person and that the Holy Spirit heard what you said? I doubt you would hold unforgiveness toward another if you saw that your sins put Jesus on the cross. Can you sin? Yes, but only if you believe a lie. If you are struggling with sin, what is the lie you believe? What part of your old man are you dragging around with you? It's not healthy to drag around dead things.

This lie is a massive stronghold in the church. If you view yourself as a sinner, it will become a self-fulfilling prophecy. You don't expect yourself to be holy, and you feel perpetually condemned by God. If you view yourself as a saint, accepted by the Father, you will live with the standard of holiness as your expectation.

> *And God raised us up with Christ and seated us with him in the heavenly realms in Christ Jesus* (Ephesians 2:6).

I will behave much differently if I believe myself to be a saint, holy, and seated with Him in heavenly realms as opposed to being just a sinner saved by grace.

God is only good sometimes (Lie).

If you asked yourself, "Is God always good to me in every situation?" What would be your answer? If you can't give an unqualified yes to this question, then you are partnering with a devastating lie. Any time you face a crisis in finances, work, health, or relationships, there's going to be a part of you that will doubt that God always has your good in mind.

> *The angel of the Lord encamps all around those who fear Him, and delivers them. Oh, taste and see that the Lord is good; blessed is the man who trusts in him! Oh, fear the Lord, you his saints! There is no want to those who fear him* (Psalm 34:7-9 NKJV).

This lie breeds doubt and unbelief and is an important cause of anxiety and depression. My elderly patient above believed this lie as well as the lie of not being fully forgiven, which caused his double-mindedness.

Sometimes life is painful and difficult, and the concept that God is always good does not feel true. God's goodness, however, far surpasses our circumstances. Just because life is difficult doesn't mean that God is not with us.

> *"For I know the plans I have for you," declares the Lord, "plans to prosper you and not to harm you, plans to give you hope and a future"* (Jeremiah 29:11).

I'm in hardship, so I must be out of God's will (Lie).

Actually, the chances are pretty good that the opposite is true. I have discovered that God is extremely interested in my character and substantially less interested in my comfort. God uses trials to train up our weak areas and give us battle experience. Some things we learn through reading or hearing; and other things are only learned by real life application.

> *Consider it pure joy, my brothers and sisters, whenever you face trials of many kinds, because you know that the testing of your faith produces perseverance. Let perseverance finish its work so that you may be mature and complete, not lacking anything* (James 1:2-4).

Trials can come to us through several means. Sometimes they come because we are reaping the fruit of our poor choices. The devil gets blamed for a lot of things we bring on ourselves due to poor planning or decision making. Other times trials come because we live on a fallen earth, and we have an enemy who seeks our destruction. And sometimes our loving Father brings us trials because He loves us and is trying to train us for service to Him. Regardless of the source, all difficulties can be used by God to bring about a good purpose in us—even the trials brought about by our own mistakes.

If you are in a difficult season, go to the Father and ask Him what He wants you to learn through this. You already know He has your good in mind and that *"all things God works for the good of those who love him, who have been called according to his purpose"* (Rom. 8:28). You also know that *"in all these things we are more than conquerors through him who loved us"* (Rom. 8:37).

When I face a crisis, I make it a point to ask Papa what it is He wants to teach me. Because I believe He is always good and His power and His ways greatly surpass anything Satan can dream up, I know I am safe in Him. Is this a time to ask for the mountain to be removed? Or is this a time to ask for wisdom and strength to find the way over the mountain? I don't know what to do if I don't know Him. No matter what, I know I can praise God in all things, and I know that I am in His will.

I am not good enough or there is something I lack (Lie).

This is a common lie that we all get caught in at some level because it has an element of truth. We believe this lie when we look at our weaknesses and forget:

> *My grace is sufficient for you, for my power is made perfect in weakness* (2 Corinthians 12:9).

The truth is that it's not about our skills, talents, or powers. The truth is:

> *I can do all this through him who gives me strength* (Philippians 4:13).

The focus has to be on Him. He is good enough, and he lacks nothing. *What would you do if you weren't afraid?*

I must always say yes (Lie).

Actually, *no* is a good word. *No* is what protects our ability to do what God wants us to do. Just because someone we love or respect asks us to do something, our response should not be an automatic yes. Jesus Himself modeled *no* with very little ambiguity or apparent regret. The companion lie to "I must say yes," is *love means I must rescue you from the consequences of your actions.*" This lie is tethered to an underlying deeper lie that says, "I do not trust that God will take care of you, so I need to be a god to you."

God does not fully love me (Lie).

This lie is the greatest lie of all, and if we look deep enough it is the root lie of all other lies.

> *For I am convinced that neither death, nor life, nor angels, nor principalities, nor things present, nor things to come, nor powers, nor height, nor depth, nor any other created thing, will be able to separate us from the love of God, which is in Christ Jesus our Lord* (Romans 8:38-39 NASB).

When we do not fully comprehend this truth that Paul writes, we will believe lies about our identity, purpose, ability to overcome, and our future. If you really believed that Jesus was crazy in love with you, viewed you as holy, would die for you, would seat you in heavenly places with Him, and would pursue you to the ends of the earth for all time, how could you believe any of the other lies? The reason we believe God is not always good is because we don't understand how much He loves us and who we are in Him. How could we possibly think we are out of His will and that somehow the trial we are in is His way of punishing us? How could we believe our loving Father would let us fail because of our weaknesses? He is not surprised by our weakness. However, He is surprised by our lack of faith. This lack of faith is directly tied to the fact that we do not comprehend His love for us.

There are numerous other lies we can believe as well. As you spend time meditating on Scripture and getting to know your loving Father, ask Him to expose the lies. Then wash your mind in His word and let Him renew your thinking.

ACTION POINTS

1. Purpose to know God, as to know Him is to know the truth. You will get to know Him as you meditate on what He says and by spending time in His presence. Here are some good Scriptures to review. Let the word wash your mind until the Scripture *feels* true to you.

   - Psalms 119:160

   - Job 23:12

   - Jeremiah 15:16

   - 1 John 1:9

   - Romans 8:9

   - Psalms 34:7-9

   - James 1:2-4

   - Romans 8:37

   - Romans 8:28

   - Jeremiah 29:11

   - 1 Corinthians 2:9

   - Romans 8:38-39

   - Ephesians 2:6

2. Read through the lies above and check to see if any of these lies *feel* true to you. If so, find the companion Scripture that speaks the truth to each of these lies and meditate on the Scripture until it renews your mind.

3. The lies about identity (we are sinners rather than saints) and about God's love are the most vital to remove. If you can get the truth seated in these two strongholds of your mind, many other lies will

automatically get knocked out and replaced with truth. So focus your attention there first.

4.   As you spend time in prayer, ask the Father to reveal other lies that you believe. Then find the corresponding truth in Scripture and repeat step two above.

Chapter 5

Take Every Thought Captive

"Worry is a cycle of inefficient thoughts
whirling around a center of fear."
—CORRIE TEN BOOM

N ow that you have exchanged lies for truth, this next chapter describes one of the most core disciplines required to move you from a lifestyle of anxiety and depression to one of peace and joy. People who live a lifestyle of peace and joy purposefully take their thoughts captive. It is critical to remember that thoughts don't go into captivity voluntarily. The essence of this chapter is to get you to look at the underlying thoughts that generate your feelings and to give you permission to flush thoughts that set themselves up against the knowledge of God and are not obedient to Christ. The beauty of this discipline is that you can do it even when you don't *feel* like it. Too many Christians let their thoughts take them down pathways they were never meant to travel. You can say *no* to certain thoughts, and you can direct your mind to think about whatsoever things are lovely, pure, admirable, praiseworthy, etc.

Before I discuss thoughts, let's review feelings again because this is where people get stuck. Although real and valuable, emotions don't necessarily reflect the truth. Feelings are difficult to control until the thoughts behind the emotions change, and this can take time. Sometimes it takes a minute or two for your feelings to come in line with your thoughts, but in a panic attack it can take substantially longer. This delay between thoughts and feelings is where people get lost. Sometimes you must use your spirit to tell your brain what to think repeatedly. The more frequently you practice this discipline, the easier it becomes and the quicker your feelings line up with your thoughts. In a later chapter, I describe a very difficult time where I camped on this discipline to survive. I could not afford to let my thoughts go down certain pathways that overwhelmed me with feelings of fear and hopelessness. I forced my brain to think about the truth, and I put the truth on my lips and spoke it into the atmosphere. As I took my thoughts captive, the fear and worry turned into hope and peace.

> *We demolish arguments and every pretension that sets itself up against the knowledge of God, and we take captive every thought to make it obedient to Christ* (2 Corinthians 10:5).

Fortunately, we were not told to take our feelings captive. Did you notice that Paul didn't say to not be angry? Instead, he warned us of the sinful actions that could arise from this negative emotion. He also addressed the need to deal with the underlying thought processes so that the anger was dealt with the same day. Our feelings are a reliable indicator of our thoughts. Think of them as the fruit of a particular tree or the temperature gauge of a system. Feelings tell you if something is off. Bill Johnson says that if you control your thoughts you don't have to worry about controlling your tongue. When you control your thoughts, your feelings and actions will follow suit. If I am feeling anxious or fearful, I better take a good look at the thought patterns that are causing these emotions.

I have a friend, and you probably do as well, who consistently lives her life based out of feelings. She will deliberately make a decision that she knows to be disobedient, but she justifies the action because of how she feels. Her life is chaotic, financially unstable, and full of painful relationships. Her inability to take her thoughts captive and her willingness to allow feelings to reign supreme have reaped destruction. Anxiety and depression are frequent visitors, and this is due to her unwillingness to renew her mind.

We need to take a proactive role in our thought life. No one else can control our thoughts but us. When we feel anxious or fearful, this is a sign that we need to examine our thoughts. Do our thoughts line up with the knowledge of God and are they obedient to Christ? If not, our next step is to repent for unsanctified thoughts and consciously demolish them. I compare it to doing laundry. Before I put the clothes in the washing machine, I get out my stain remover and hold the laundry up to the light. If I see a stain, I spray it thoroughly. I don't want that clothing to come out of the wash still dirty. We need to do the same thing with our thoughts, holding them up into the light of Scripture and spraying them with the truth. In other words, I wash my thoughts with the truth of the Word of God. I may have to do this several times to get the thought captive.

Some thoughts are not worth having, and they need to be flushed. Just because you have a thought doesn't mean you have to cozy up to it. If I have an ungodly thought, I consciously say to myself, "I reject that thought. It does not belong to me, and I refuse to own it." I then picture myself flushing that thought down the drain, disassociating myself from the lie. Then I purposefully set my thoughts on what God says about the situation. This is the truth *I choose* to believe. I may not feel it, but I choose truth anyway. The feelings come into alignment eventually.

If you haven't done this, it takes a bit of practice, and the key is consistency. Havilah Cunnington compares it to putting a two-year-old to bed. You put them to bed, and they come out again. You put them to bed, and they come out again. You may have to put them to bed several times until they stay there, and you may have to get quite firm. You don't just say, "Okay, I guess you can stay up. You win. Come on, let's cuddle on the couch."

But how often do we do that with our thoughts? We put them away, but then we let them out again. In fact, we cozy right up to them and hold them close. It takes work, practice, and a conscious choice to take your thoughts captive. But only you can do it. The good thing is that the more you do it, the easier it becomes. If you are consistent with discipline, the two-year-old learns he has to stay in bed. The same can be said of your thoughts. Let me also add that the quicker and more frequently you practice this discipline, the easier it is to be successful. When you let your thoughts run rampant and your feelings are full blown, you have to work harder to get your thoughts lined up. When you catch the thought in its earliest form, before it's had a chance to wreak havoc on your emotions, the easier it is to think about the truth.

Much of our thought life is subconscious. I compare it to an iceberg, which is 90 percent underwater and unseen. The visible part of the iceberg that is seen is only 10 percent of its total size. We too are only consciously aware of a small percentage of our thoughts unless we tune in and examine them. The majority of our thought life is subconscious, which is typically what gets us into trouble. These subconscious thoughts can generate feelings of worry, fear, anger, sadness, etc. This is where feelings come in handy because they are telling us about our thoughts. The trick is to not get lost in the feelings and accept them as the truth. Instead, examine the thoughts and actively replace the lies with truth.

I want to point out that feelings come and go, but they don't necessarily reflect the truth. Even though something *feels* true, it doesn't make it so.

FEELINGS ARE A RELIABLE INDICATOR OF YOUR THOUGHTS, BUT NOT OF TRUTH!

So many people operate out of what they feel and not out of truth. I love my husband, but that doesn't mean I always *feel* loving toward him. When he does something that irritates me, do my feelings of irritation mean that I don't love him? Of course not. If I operated out of feelings, I would be double-minded, all over the place. My emotions don't change the truth of my love for him or my actions toward him. As I set my thoughts on all of the wonderful things I love about my husband and the wonderful memories we share, my emotions quickly change to those of love and affection. In other words, my thoughts control my feelings, not vice versa.

It is important to have congruence between our thoughts and feelings. For something to be true to you, you must believe it to be so. It is not enough to *know* or recite the word. You must *believe* the word for it to feel true. Unfortunately, I am acquainted with many unbelieving believers. These are people who know the doctrine of salvation and God's love, but it does not feel true to them. They can recite the Scriptures from memory, but it does not penetrate their heart and mind because they do not believe it to be true.

CONGRUENCE BETWEEN YOUR MIND AND SPIRIT

Another thing to remember is that we have an enemy. He can be very subtle, and he comes to us with thoughts and suggestions that are mixed with truth and they feel like our very own ideas. Because there is truth mixed in with these thoughts, we often accept them as our own, not realizing that their origin is demonic. Sometimes all the enemy has to do is remind us of a past injustice or failure, and we allow ourselves to go down the path of that past event, regenerating all of the original negative emotions. This is a frequent technique used by the enemy to get us to feel a negative emotion—bitterness, anger, failure, etc.—over something we've already taken care of. Or at least we thought we did! If we find ourselves feeling angry over a past injustice, we then feel guilty. Then the enemy tells us that our forgiveness was not genuine and that we are a hypocrite. What we don't realize is that we've just been slimed. He brings a thought to us. We neglect to hold that thought up to the obedience of Christ, and instead of rejecting the thought we embrace it as true. We allow that thought to run its course and give birth to all of those negative emotions because we didn't take it captive from the beginning.

If you find yourself feeling angry and guilty on a frequent basis, there is a good chance you've been sucked into this cycle. Taking your thoughts captive is much easier when you wear your salvation helmet, described in a later chapter. Our salvation helmet protects our mind from the onslaught of demonic thoughts. When you hold that thought up to the light of the knowledge of God and the obedience of Christ, is it true?

WHAT IS THE MOTIVATION BEHIND THE THOUGHT?

"For I know the plans I have for you," declares the Lord, "plans to prosper you and not to harm you, plans to give you hope and a future" (Jeremiah 29:11).

How do you know the origin of the thought? The motivation behind all of God's thoughts for us is love. God loves His children, and He does not abuse them. His intent for us is restoration, wholeness, hope, and life. If your thoughts make you feel condemned, hopeless, inadequate, or unloved, then they are not coming from the Holy Spirit.

Although Satan does not have authority, he does have power when we come into agreement with Him. This is why we have to renew our minds and take our thoughts captive. Our thought life fuels the invisible realm—evil or heavenly. Bill Johnson states we create alliances by what we choose to think about. This is the reason Jesus rebuked Peter and said *get behind me, Satan*. He recognized that Peter was promoting thoughts that did not come from the heavenly realm, even though what Peter said seemed reasonable to the natural mind.

What kingdom are you fueling with your thought life?

ACTION POINTS

1. What do these Scriptures say about God's love and faithfulness toward us?

    _____

    _____

    _____

    _____

    _____

2. When you examine the origin of your thoughts that don't line up with the knowledge of God and the obedience of Christ, what is Satan trying to get you to agree with?

    _____

    _____

    _____

    _____

    _____

3. What is the truth you need to apply, i.e., what should your spirit tell your mind to think instead?

_____

_____

_____

_____

_____

4. When the old thought patterns come out again, don't become discouraged. Remember the two year-old who needs to be put back to bed until he stays there. Repeat the process above and apply the truth. Once you apply the truth of the word long enough, it can remove any stain.

MEDITATION SCRIPTURES

- Psalms 86:15
- 1 John 4:7-8
- 1 John 4:16
- Zephaniah 3:17
- Jeremiah 29:11
- Galatians 2:20
- Psalms 34:4
- Isaiah 41:10
- Psalms 9:9-10
- Psalms 2:3-6

Chapter 6

Forgiveness

*"Forgiveness is the fragrance that the violet
sheds on the heel that has crushed it."*
—OLD ADAGE

Now that we've identified lies and have taken our thoughts captive, we come to an area that is a huge stumbling block for many. Having talked to numerous patients over the years, I have discovered that one of the most common causes of anxiety and depression is bitterness and anger over past injustice. Bitterness and anger are the fruits produced from an unwillingness to forgive. In an earlier chapter, we discussed the trees (neural pathways) that we allow to grow in our mind. The two main trees were described as the Tree of Faith and the Tree of Unbelief. These trees do not flourish together. One will always dominate the other. In addition, there is another tree we can allow to grow in our mind, and that is the Tree of Offense. This tree is particularly poisonous to the "soil" of our mind. The Tree of Unbelief flourishes in the contaminated soil produced by the Tree of Offense. In contrast, the Tree of Faith will be permanently stunted and weak if the Tree of Offense is growing in our mind. The Tree of Offense begins from the seed of unforgiveness that grows when we are unwilling to forgive ourselves, others, or God.

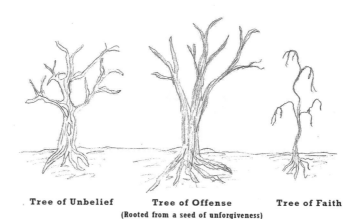

Tree of Unbelief   **Tree of Offense**   **Tree of Faith**
(Rooted from a seed of unforgiveness)

Several years ago someone close to me offended me dearly. I went to my friend in the biblical manner outlined by Jesus in Matthew 18:21, but this person was unrepentant. My friend could not see that what they had done was wrong and did not care that they had caused me grief. Day by day, the offense grew larger in my mind. I stewed over this incident for several months, and it caused me tremendous emotional distress. I would not forgive my friend, so the Tree of Offense grew quite large. This tree began to produce toxic fruit, and I found myself irritable and lacking joy. I nursed my hurt, not realizing that what I meant for another was poisoning me. My stubbornness stunted my Tree of Faith, which was then unable to produce the fruits of joy and peace. I knew I needed to forgive, but my friend did not deserve it!

It's easier to forgive someone when they say they are sorry. However, forgiveness is often difficult when the person you need to forgive is unrepentant. I still remember the moment when I prayed and spoke forgiveness to my friend for what they had done. I felt a huge weight lift off my mind and my spirit. The irritability and anger left. My joy and peace returned. I had plucked this poisonous tree from the soil in my mind, and the Tree of Faith could now produce the fruits of joy and peace.

TREE OF FAITH

To forgive is to set a prisoner free and discover that the prisoner was you. —LEWIS B. SMEDES

I had held my friend as a prisoner in my mind. My friend did not deserve freedom, as they were not sorry for what they had done. In addition, my friend did not care that they had hurt me. So I kept my friend locked up for months. In reality, I was the one locked up. Once I let my friend go, I was set free.

Robert, an elderly man who had been my patient for many years, recently died of heart disease. Although he stated that he was a Christian, I saw no fruits of the spirit growing in Robert's life. Instead, this man abundantly displayed the ugly fruits of anger, bitterness, and hatred. Robert was depressed and spoke bitterly about his wife, who had left him years ago, and his grown children who would have nothing to do with him. This man blamed everyone else for his problems. He could not see that his bitterness and rage had caused the ones he loved to flee. Admittedly, Robert had a rough upbringing. His father abandoned the family when he was five years old, and his mother had been an alcoholic. To make matters worse, he was molested by an uncle. These traumas had caused much offense and he was unwilling to let them go. His unforgiveness grew into a very large and dominant Tree of Offense. The fruits of bitterness and rage that this tree produced contaminated every area of his life.

Have you ever tried to peer through a thick, wavy piece of glass? What you see is distorted and looks nothing like its true appearance. Robert viewed the world through the thick, wavy glass of bitterness. This prevented him from seeing that his behaviors were the cause of his divorce and family estrangement. Unfortunately, Robert had allowed the Tree of Offense to grow for many years, and this tree was so large that nothing good could grow in the garden of his mind. The older he grew, the more twisted his thinking became. He died a very lonely, embittered man. You probably know people like Robert. There are no medications to treat bitterness. The only thing that would have put Robert on the path to freedom was to forgive those who had hurt him; sadly, he chose not to do this.

Bitterness and peace do not exist together. You cannot hold unforgiveness against others and expect to feel joyful. Whatever tree you allow to grow in your mind will produce its corresponding fruit. If you are feeling irritable, angry, or sad, check to see if you have the Tree of Offense growing in your thought life. Who are you withholding forgiveness from—God, another person, yourself? Sometimes the offense happened long ago, or it started quite small and you may have ignored it or blown it off as being silly. Take care of it anyway.

As I said earlier, it's easy to forgive when someone tells you they are sorry. But what about situations where there is no repentance? What if the insult or injury was unprovoked and caused you great emotional or physical pain? What we have to remember is that Christ forgave us while we were yet sinners. We did not *deserve* forgiveness. It was given freely to us.

But if you do not forgive, neither will your Father in heaven forgive your trespasses (Mark 11:26 NKJV).

When Peter asked Jesus how often he had to forgive his brother who had sinned against him, Jesus told him seventy times seven. Then Jesus went on to tell a story about a wealthy man who was owed a substantial amount of money by one of his servants. The wealthy man was going to have his servant thrown into jail, but when the man asked for forgiveness the wealthy man showed him mercy and forgave his debt. Then this servant went out and discovered that he was owed a few dollars by another man. Yet when the man who owed the money asked for forgiveness, the servant would not give it to him and had him thrown in jail. When the wealthy man found out what his servant had done, he was furious and threw his servant in prison (see Matt. 18:23-35). How could his servant who was forgiven much be unwilling to forgive a small amount?

Sometimes, we are just like this servant. We have been forgiven much! Jesus willingly sacrificed Himself for us so that we might be forgiven. How then can we possibly think we have the "right" to not forgive another? None of us *deserves* forgiveness. I know that I am incapable of doing anything that would justify Christ dying for me on the cross. How about you? We don't want to be like the servant who was forgiven much, and yet ourselves be unwilling to forgive others. It just doesn't end well.

Forgiveness is me giving up my right to hurt you for hurting me. —ANONYMOUS

As you are reading this, you may be thinking, "I know I need to forgive myself, but I just can't do it. I've done something so awful, I know I deserve to be punished and how can I just let it go?" Or, "You have no idea the horror that was done to me. I was just a child and those who were supposed to protect me abused me. Where was God anyway? How can I possibly forgive?"

Angie, a 32-year-old mother with two children, has been my patient for several years now. She is full of joy, but this wasn't always the case. I discovered that Angie grew up with a mother who was a drug addict and had numerous men in the house, some of whom had molested her. Her mother knew about the abuse but was unwilling to intervene because she wanted the money for drugs. Angie eventually entered into foster care and met Jesus while attending a youth group. Up until this point, Angie was both anxious and depressed, tormented by her past, angry with her mother, and the men who had hurt her. However, a transformation began to occur as she forgave her mother and the men who had abused her. Angie changed from a young woman who was depressed and anxious to someone who had hope and joy. She attended college and married a wonderful young man and has not had a recurrence of the anxiety or depression. I asked Angie how she was able to do this. She told me that as she realized how much Jesus truly loved her and had forgiven her she too must forgive. No one told her to do this, but she knew in her spirit she must forgive. It was a choice she made. Angie has not forgotten what was done to her, but it no longer holds her hostage.

Just because we forgive does not mean we forget. Angie's mother still lives a destructive lifestyle, and although Angie loves her mother she keeps healthy boundaries so that she and her children are not harmed by the choices of her mother. Just because she has forgiven her mother doesn't mean her mother has permission to come into her life and wreak havoc.

I am very careful about what I say to my friend who caused me great pain. I have forgiven them, but I would not trust them with certain information as this would be foolish. Even though I feel no resentment, my friend would need to regain my trust before I placed myself in a vulnerable position with them again. I have changed my boundaries with this person, and this is a necessary and healthy thing to do.

Sometimes we withhold forgiveness from ourselves, as we feel we need to be punished for what we've done. I can say after talking to many people—you will never be able to punish yourself enough. You won't wake up one morning and say, "Okay, I've served my time." The truth is that Christ did it all for us on the cross. There isn't one thing you can add to the cross, and it's both foolish and arrogant to think you can do so. If you have genuinely repented and made amends as best you can (regardless of the response of the offended party), then it's done. Christ has forgiven you, and that is enough.

Not only has He forgiven you, but He will not remind you of your sin. As far as He is concerned it's as though it never happened. David speaks about the loving kindness and compassion of God and says this: *"As far as the east is from the west, so far has he removed our transgressions from us"* (Ps. 103:12). Think about that. How far is the east from the west? East and west are opposites. Our sin is opposite from us—so far removed, it no longer touches our life.

Are you being reminded of and tormented by your past sins, things you've repented more than once? You are not alone. Bringing up the past is a common tactic of the enemy. It's one of his favorite and frequently used schemes. These thoughts are not coming from God but from another spirit realm that is demonic in nature. How do we know for sure? The Apostle Paul said:

Therefore, there is now no condemnation for those who are in Christ Jesus, because through Christ Jesus the law of the Spirit who gives life has set you free from the law of sin and death (Romans 8:1-2).

When we repent, we no longer live under the law. We live in "Grace-land." Before the cross, we lived under the law. We now live on the other side of the cross in a new covenant. To go back to the law is the equivalent of saying the cross was inadequate.

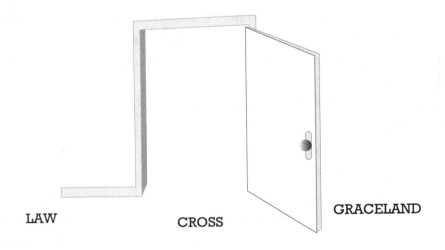

LAW   CROSS   GRACELAND

When tormenting thoughts come to our minds, we have both the right and the authority to place these thoughts under the obedience of Christ. In fact, we are commanded to do so. The enemy is our accuser. So if our thoughts make us feel ashamed or condemned, we know the source is demonic. How do we know for sure?

And so we know and rely on the love God has for us. God is love. Whoever lives in love lives in God, and God in them. This is how love is made complete among us so that we will have confidence on the day of judgment: In this world we are like Jesus. There is no fear in love. But perfect love drives out fear, because fear has to do with punishment. The one who fears is not made perfect in love (1 John 4:16-18).

God loves us thoroughly, and His love is so complete that it drives out fear. I love my children immensely, and I know that God loves me more than I could ever love my boys. When my kids were little and they did something wrong and made amends, I was satisfied with their repentance. My boys did not worry that I was going to continue to bring up the past and repeatedly punish them. That would be a form of child abuse. I suspect you are the same with your own children. If we who are earthly can love and forgive our kids, how much more does God do so for us? God does not abuse His children.

The enemy is a clever liar. Often what he says has an element of truth, but it's never the *complete* truth. When he reminds us of past failures, we get caught in the trap of agreeing with him that what we've done was wrong. That part of the thought is true. But I've never had the enemy remind me of the *greater* truth—that I was completely forgiven by what Jesus did on the cross, and that my sins are removed from me as far as the east is from the west. Which is the *greater* truth—our sin or Christ's forgiveness? *Not all truth is equal!*

Perhaps you are holding God hostage to a past offense. Why did God allow your child to die of cancer? Where was God when your brother was killed by a drunk driver? If God loved you, why did He let these things happen? Can you trust Him?

These are real questions we ask when we suffer pain. Our human nature wants answers, and we want someone or something to blame. I will be the first to say that I do not have all the answers. But I do know that God thinks differently than I do, and He sees the end from the beginning. Most of the time I just see the part I'm in, and I only see it from my perspective. I don't know about you, but there is a lot about God I don't understand. Like Paul, I *"see through a glass, darkly"* (1 Cor. 13:12 KJV).

I also know that *"in all things God works for the good of those who love him, who have been called according to his purpose"* (Rom. 8:28). It may not be good now, but it will be at some point. God has a way of redeeming horrible things and bringing good out of them. I've seen it over and over again. This does not mean God caused your pain, but He can redeem it. God is always good to us. Even God's discipline is meant for our good and not our punishment. I say this to make the point that God is not the source of bad things in our life. It is the enemy who is determined to destroy us.

Pamela, a 41-year-old divorced woman, came to see me as a new patient who had moved to the area and needed to refill her antidepressant medications. Her history revealed a sad story of sexual molestation at the age of six, difficulty with school, a failed marriage, and lifelong depression and anxiety. Pamela moved to Redding to attend our church and was seeking freedom from the past that haunted her. When I asked her about her relationship with God, she admitted there was a barrier that kept her from trusting God. Pamela had been to years and years of counseling with little benefit. I encouraged her to make an appointment with a Sozo counselor at our church. *Sozo* is a Greek word that means *saved, healed, and delivered,* referring to the fact that our salvation is multifaceted and isn't just limited to the salvation of our soul.

A few months later Pamela came in to see me and her countenance had been completely transformed from sad and tense to beaming. She wanted to stop her antidepressants because she didn't think she needed them any longer. I was a bit skeptical. This patient had a 20-year history of major depressive disorder and had been on medications for most of that time. So I asked her what had changed. She told me she had met with a Sozo prayer counselor and had told her about the barrier that kept her from trusting God. During the prayer session, she asked the Holy Spirit to come and reveal the source of the barrier. The Holy Spirit took Pamela back to a memory of the very first time she was molested. She could see herself as a little girl, in the very room with the stepfather where it happened. This memory was quite painful for Pamela, but the prayer counselor asked her to look around and see who else was in the room. As Pamela looked over to a corner, she saw that Jesus was standing there. The counselor asked her what Jesus was doing, and as Pamela looked closely she saw that Jesus was crying. At this point, Pamela burst into sobs. She now understood that she had never been alone. Jesus had always been with her, and He was terribly grieved about what had been done to her. She was then able to see other situations where Jesus had protected her and brought her into a relationship with Him. Pamela immediately let go of her offense toward God and the barrier of not being able to trust vanished. I agreed to wean Pamela off of the medication. It's been five years and there has been no recurrence of the anxiety or depression for this patient. What years of counseling were unable to accomplish, the Holy Spirit did in minutes.

> When you forgive, you in no way change the past—but you sure do change the future. —Bernard Meltzer

Are you ready to let go of the offenses that are holding you hostage? Are you willing to let God be the one who deals justly with those who have hurt you so that you no longer have to be the punisher? Some very good friends of mine, Barry and Lori Byrne, developed a Forgiveness Tool for the workshops they teach, and it can be found in their *Nothing Hidden Tool Booklet*. I have their permission to share this practical tool with you. I strongly recommend this resource that has many other tools to bring you freedom in relationships.

FORGIVENESS TOOL[1]

This tool is an aid in helping you lead yourself or another person through forgiveness. If you're leading another person, have them participate with you in adding things that they need to forgive.

True forgiveness goes beyond simply forgiving someone for their behavior and the wrong they did. Forgiveness involves forgiving someone for all of the hurt and pain they have caused, as well as the effects of those hurts in your life.

Count on the Holy Spirit releasing prophetic words and discernment to you beyond your own understanding. Step out, take a risk, and watch what the Holy Spirit will do with these steps:

1. Father God, thank you for forgiving me for all my sins. Because of your forgiveness, I also forgive (person's name).

2. (Person's name), I forgive you for the lies the enemy brought to me as a result of your actions or words.

Listen to the Holy Spirit and say the lies as they come.

Lies about:

_____ Myself...

_____ My relationships...

_____ My view of men/women...

_____ My view of marriage...

_____ My view of motherhood/fatherhood...

_____ My view of God...

_____ (Other)...

*3. (Person's name), **I forgive you for bringing fear into my life.** (For example: Fear of intimacy, failure, being alone, death, not being enough, fear of man—these are just some examples. Listen to what the Holy Spirit is saying about **this** situation.)*

Fear of _____

Fear of _____

Fear of _____ ..., *etc.*

4. (Person's name), **I forgive you for opening the door to:**
*(For example: Anger, self-hatred, passivity, accusation, feelings of worthlessness, shame, self-protection, sexual perversion, shutting down, depression, the occult—these are just some examples. Listen to what the Holy Spirit is saying about **this** situation.)*

Opening the door to _____

Opening the door to _____

Opening the door to _____ ..., *etc.*

5. (Person's name), **I forgive you for the lack of:** *(For example: Protection, love, nurturing, relationship, knowing me, affection, attention, care, stability, etc.—these are just some examples. Listen to what the Holy Spirit is saying about **this** situation.)*

Lack of _____

Lack of _____

Lack of _____ ..., *etc.*

6. (Person's name), I forgive you for all of the pain and sufferings that I've had to deal with (throughout my life) because of what you did.

7. Pray and bless the person you just forgave.

Let me be honest. Forgiveness is not easy, and we often do it out of obedience, not because we feel like doing it. This is why it took me so long to extend forgiveness to my friend. I didn't feel compassion for my friend but forgave strictly because I knew I had sinned. If you are waiting until you "feel" like forgiving, you could wait forever. We don't live out of feelings but out of truth.

Because feelings follow thoughts, I've learned to forgive repeatedly until my feelings line up with my thoughts. I might have to declare forgiveness seventy times seven, but I do so until I feel the truth of that forgiveness resonate in my soul. If it's a simple offense, I might be able to forgive easily, but deep offenses usually require several rounds of truth application!

So what do you do when you forgive and a few days later you find yourself ruminating on the past offense again? (Remember, this pathway has probably been traveled on repeatedly and is still physically present in your brain.) You feel the same hurt and anger all again, and now you have the additional guilt of feeling like your original forgiveness was false. This is a common tactic of the enemy. He reminds you of your past offense, and you agree to think about it again. Then he condemns you for thinking about it and tells you that you are a hypocrite. It's a clever scheme.

Once I discovered this, I went on the offensive. Now, if I find myself thinking about a past offense I first say no to the train of thought. Then I thank Satan for reminding me that I have forgiven this person. I thank him for reminding me of how much God loves me. I thank him for reminding me that Jesus paid everything on the cross, and I'm so glad that my sins are far removed from me. Then I turn it around and begin to pray for God to bless the person I've forgiven. I find my thoughts and feelings quickly turn around. I have done this so consistently that the demonic realm rarely bothers me with past offenses .

Now is the time to pluck those Trees of Offense out of your life. Don't let yourself be held hostage by the past. This personal study below will take you through the process. Freedom is waiting for you!

ACTION POINTS

1. Do you feel angry, bitter, resentful, unworthy, fearful, or sad?

_____

_____

_____

_____

2. Do you have the Tree of Offense growing in your mind? If so, who do you hold hostage to unforgiveness? Yourself? Another? God?

_____

_____

_____

_____

3. Use the forgiveness tool above and apply it to any situation that you described above. You may need to use this tool repeatedly. There is no guilt in that. You need to create new neural pathways in your brain that will override the past offense. The goal is to forgive until your feelings line up with the truth.

4. Are you being tormented by past offenses that you thought you'd genuinely forgiven? Is the enemy making you feel dirty and ashamed? Go ahead and forgive the person again and then go on the offensive. Joyfully thank satan for reminding you of how much you have been forgiven. Remind him that Christ paid everything on the cross and your sins are far removed from you.

5. Then begin to bless the person who offended you. Do this until you feel the return of your peace. Remember that Satan is sneaky and he's been successful with this tactic in the past and will try it again. Just be

consistent and he will leave. *"Resist the devil, and he will flee from you"* (James 4:7).

MEDITATION SCRIPTURES

- Mark 11:26
- Psalms 103:12
- Romans 8
- 1 John 4

NOTE

1. Barry and Lori Byrne, *Nothing Hidden Ministries Tool Booklet* (Living Strong, 2015).

Chapter 7

No Is a Healthy Word: Setting Boundaries

"A 'No' uttered from the deepest conviction is better than a 'Yes' merely uttered to please, or worse, to avoid trouble."
—MAHATMA GANDHI

This chapter is closely linked to the lies we believe about ourselves, God, and our identity. The inability to say *no* and to set healthy boundaries is a powerful and chronic stressor for many people, often resulting in anxiety or depression. Although *no* is not a bad word, many of us are reluctant to use it. Protecting our emotional resources, finances, time, and physical health is our responsibility alone, and *no* helps us do that. *No* is what keeps us from carrying burdens and responsibilities that don't belong to us.

Emily, a 47-year-old woman, has seen me for several years. Her typical appearance is one of exhaustion and resignation. She manages the book-keeping for her husband's business, works another job full time, and has three teenagers at home. Although her husband has two other siblings, he has just invited his ailing mother to live in their home, against Emily's wishes, and Emily finds herself caring for her mother-in-law as well. Her husband is involved in car shows, and he expects Emily to attend the shows with him most Saturdays. She has no interest or time for car shows, but to avoid his displeasure she attends, and this makes her feel resentful. She tells me she has no choice and must say yes to everyone but herself. When I ask her why she doesn't just say no, she looks at me like I've grown two heads. I can tell, that *saying no* is a foreign concept to Emily.

People who find it difficult to set boundaries often struggle with low self-esteem and are looking for acceptance from others. Because they don't realize their identity in Christ, they look for identity through being "needed." Their dependency on others for acceptance attracts or creates relationships where others take advantage of them for their needs, creating unhealthy cycles of codependency. An excellent resource that I recommend for people struggling with this issue is *Boundaries* by Cloud and Townsend.

As you think about Emily what are the real choices that she could pose to her husband? First, Emily could tell her husband she can either do his books or work full time but not both, and they could choose together which would be best for their family. Emily could tell her husband she does not enjoy the car shows and would decide based on other family obligations whether or not to attend with no guilt. Emily also has the choice to determine whether or not to care for her mother-in-law in her home. If the answer is no, then her husband needs to respect her decision and find another option. If the decision is yes, then Emily can require that in-home help—housekeeping, gardening—must be provided by another as she will not have time to do both. Her husband may not like these choices, but these are legitimate and reasonable options that Emily can exercise.

Jesus had no problem saying *no* without any apparent difficulty or feelings of guilt. The Pharisees asked Him for a sign, and He refused (see Matt. 12:38-39). On another occasion, under questioning by Herod, Jesus declined to answer (see Luke 23:9). I wonder how many of us would have the courage to refuse our spiritual and governmental leaders? Jesus firmly rebuked not only leaders but one of His dearest friends quite harshly. When Peter questioned the plan outlined by Jesus for the upcoming crucifixion, Jesus said, "Get behind me, Satan!" (Mark 8:33). Now, that's a firm *no!* Jesus wasn't always nice. He had strong boundaries. How many of us would go into a public area and chase people out with a whip, or call our leaders a brood of vipers or whitewashed graves—to their faces, no less? Jesus was quite firm on what He would do (heal on the Sabbath) and what He wouldn't do (show off for the Pharisees or delay His journey to Jerusalem).

Another thing Jesus was unwilling to do was to rescue people from their poor choices. At the last supper, Jesus did not beg or ask Judas to change his mind about his intended betrayal. Jesus didn't try to coax people into believing in Him or following Him. People chose from their own heart as Jesus wasn't willing to try to manipulate their decision. He also knew His boundaries and had no problem telling people *no*. There were several people who said they wanted to follow Him but needed to do something else first. I know that I would consider taking care of burial arrangements for my father a high priority, but Jesus had a specific standard He was looking for and He had no problem sticking to the plan.

Jesus protected His personal time so that He could spend time with the Father and get away to rest with the disciples. He protected His priorities. When Jesus said *no* to man, it allowed Him to say *yes* to the Father. Often we have to say *no* to things that appear good to preserve our resources for the better things. When Jesus left the multitudes to get away, I suspect there were people who still needed healing. We will always have people pulling on us for "good" things, so we need to know our limits to preserve our resources for the best thing. These boundaries are different for each of us and need to be worked out between the Father and us.

Jesus knew His mission, which was to do whatever the Father was doing, and He reserved His resources for that goal. A simple example is Jesus limiting His disciples to 12. I'm sure there were others who wanted to be disciples, but I suspect Jesus knew His capacity to pour intimately into those who would carry the message after He left had limitations. And even among the twelve, His time was not spent equally. The Bible records several occasions when Jesus took only Peter, James, and John with Him and not the other nine. Jesus had an inner circle, and not everyone had equal access. I'm sure that some were disappointed and probably complained, but Jesus didn't change His plan, and we see no apologies. Again, His focus was on doing what He saw the Father do. Unfortunately, many people make decisions and open the door to their resources based on a fear of what others will think or because of wanting approval from man or because they feel a need to be fair. God is not always fair. The issue isn't *am I being fair*, but *what does God want me to do in this situation?*

The reality is that when we say *no* to the requests of man, we can then pour ourselves into the *yes* of the Father. What would your life look like if you only did what you saw the Father do?

I keep the doors to my house locked for a reason, and I suspect you do as well. The lock on my door allows me to determine who gets to come into my house and who doesn't. I also get to choose which rooms I let people go into or what closets they can open and when they need to leave. I'd be very reluctant to let someone I had just met wander through my home without permission. Only a fool would allow a stranger to have access to valuables. People I know well can go most anywhere, and family members can help themselves to anything in the cabinets or the fridge.

But there are some places in my home reserved just for myself and my husband. The point is that it's my responsibility to lock or open my door, not someone else's. And even within my home, I have different boundaries or levels of access. The person knocking doesn't get to decide. I decide. This is a simple example of a reasonable and expected boundary about protecting your physical space, but the same principle applies to relationships.

Because we all have limitations in our time, emotional/physical capacity, and financial resources, we need to keep doors that lock in each of these areas. Like Jesus, not everybody gets equal access. Just as I determine when to open my front door, I also determine how much time I am willing to commit to a certain project or activity, how much emotional energy and time I put into the people around me, and if I give to another. I don't let other people tell me what I need to give them. I alone am responsible to steward what God has given me. If I give away to another what was meant for God's call, whose fault is that? I have no right to wring my hands, blame others, and verbally complain about being "stressed" because all of my resources are being used on something God never called me to do.

There are many anxious and depressed patients who are frustrated because their time, energy, and financial resources are being used for things never intended or approved by God. They've let others come into these spaces and take whatever they'd like. Unfortunately, no matter the whining or complaining, the doors aren't going to lock themselves. Only you can lock and unlock your personal spaces. If you feel like a victim, you've only got yourself to blame. It's time to lock some doors.

Although not setting healthy boundaries occurs in both sexes, I've discovered that my female patients seem to struggle with this issue more than my male patients. I suspect that the difficulty of setting healthy boundaries may be a factor for the increased incidence of anxiety and depression in women compared to men. It's not that men don't struggle with boundaries, but it looks a bit different. Men often get their identity through their work or what they produce, and this can cause them to not set proper boundaries in these areas, leading to neglected family members.

Women are instinctive nurturers and often get approval, if not identity, through their nurturing. This was the case with Emily, who I described earlier. Women want people around them to be happy, and they somehow feel responsible for the emotional state of others. To make matters worse, women are "feelers." They have invisible antennas that pick up on the emotional states of those around them. If they suspect someone they love is struggling, they tend to ask questions and offer support. This is a good thing, but sometimes it goes too far, and they allow themselves to get sucked into other people's stuff. If they are not careful, they start carrying a load that belongs to another or God. I know this well because not only am I a mother, I'm a medical professional with people coming to me daily for help. I've been sucked into other people's stuff many times! A pearl of wisdom I've learned the hard way is that if I find myself caring more about the situation than the patient, more interested in solutions than the patient, or if I'm just a sounding board for a bunch of whining, then it's time to set some boundaries. I am not going to give away my valuable time, advice, or emotional energy to someone who sees themselves as a victim and isn't willing to do what they need to do to change their situation. If they change their mind, then I'll be there. I'm willing to shoulder as much as they are willing to shoulder but no more.

Men operate differently, at least as a general rule. Think about it. How often do the men around you ask you how you're feeling? It's just not on their radar unless it's obvious. There are both biological and cultural reasons for this difference. This is not to say that men are not nurturing, nor that they are unaware of the feelings of others, but culture does not put as much pressure on men to feel responsible for the wellbeing of people around them. Now if you asked a man to help you solve a problem, he'd be up for it, but he doesn't know how to fix your feelings. Men tend to figure that if their friend or coworker has an issue, it's their issue to bring up if they choose. They see a distinct boundary between themselves and others. It's uncommon that a male patient comes in to see me for depression because he's struggling with an adult child who is making poor choices. He might come in if he's been fired or his wife has left him, but rarely because he's caught up in other people's stuff. Yet this is a very common theme for my female patients.

Men, and I'm speaking in generalities, have an easier time differentiating their stuff from those of others. In other words, they see their family members as separate beings who can make choices for themselves and live with the consequences. They may not like the choices their loved ones make, but they don't feel guilty or responsible. Unlike women, who often feel guilty for not only the choice but the resulting consequences. There is something within in us that says, "If I had only done or said…" the outcome would have been different. The false guilt can cause women to intervene, rescue, or attempt to ameliorate consequences for others. Men may do this as well, but I see it more frequently in my female patients.

Nancy, a 48-year-old woman, came into my office seeking treatment for feeling "stressed out." She was struggling with concentration at work, irritability, and insomnia. She admitted to worrisome thoughts about her 28-year-old son, who had a methamphetamine addiction, and her struggles to "help" him. Her son was not working and lived at home without paying rent, food, utilities, or his car insurance. He also refused to help around the house, get a job, or seek treatment for his drug addiction. She and her husband had given their son 60 days to make the requested changes or leave. But it was long past 60 days, and Nancy could not get herself to follow through. As you can imagine, the difference of opinion was causing friction in their marriage and contributed to her feeling overwhelmed. Nancy was caught between wanting to help her son and wanting to please her husband. I asked Nancy how she was "helping" her son by actively supporting him in his pursuit of a destructive lifestyle. Why was she paying his expenses when he was using his resources to buy drugs? She responded, "I know. But if I don't *help* him, he will end up on the streets, and I just couldn't handle the guilt if something happened to him."

The truth came out. The motivation driving Nancy was fear disguised as love. Nancy loved her son, but not enough to do the hard thing. Living on the streets was her son's decision, and that would be an option he could choose to make or not. Her son was a 28-year-old adult who was responsible for his choices, and his decisions were no reflection of her motherhood.

Unfortunately, Nancy was more concerned about her feelings of guilt then she was about the long-term outcome for her son. Love is often tough, and it can be painful, but the genuine goal of love is to do what is best for the people around us, not appease our guilt or try to make everybody happy. Setting healthy boundaries would have been genuine love for this young man. Giving him a couple of months to get into a drug program, get a job, and pay for his expenses was reasonable. Pushing him into living as an adult, which he needed to do at 28, was not punishment but love. Unfortunately, this young man had learned that there would be no enforcement of the boundary, so he had no motivation to change his behavior. As he was unwilling to do this on his own, he needed the people around him to "love" him by requiring him to man up or face the consequences of his choices.

I wish I could say Nancy followed my advice, but up to this point she has not. Her son is deeply involved in drugs, and she and her husband are now divorced, as he was unwilling to live with the chaos in the home. No medication will take away Nancy's anxiety and "stress," as she is carrying a load that does not belong to her, and she does not have the capacity to fix the problem.

I want to differentiate between the stresses of caring for young children or for adults who are unable—not unwilling—to care for themselves. Nor am I talking about helping adult children who are pursuing drug treatment or who need assistance as they pursue their education or who may need help due to an emergency or unforeseen circumstances. These are situations where we come alongside and help carry the burden, but the *helping* shouldn't be a chronic activity. My heart goes out to families who are caring for loved ones with mental or physical disabilities, grandchildren who have unfit parents, or for frail elderly parents. Obviously, these are people God has put into our lives to nurture and watch over as we are able, and we trust Him to give us the grace to do so as they are unable to care fully for themselves.

This is where the Scripture, *"Carry each other's burdens, and in this way you will fulfill the law of Christ,"* comes into play (Gal. 6:2). Interestingly, in the very same chapter of Galatians Paul writes, *"for each one should carry their own load"* (Gal. 6:5). So which is it? Do we carry one another's burdens, or do we let them carry their load?

The answer has to do with capacity. When my children were little, I helped dress them and feed them because they did not have the ability to do so. As they grew older, I shifted more of what I "carried" for them into their hands because they were able to "carry their own load." As you can expect, I faced resistance (there's nothing like getting a ten-year-old boy to do his own laundry), but they needed to learn to carry their weight. There were many times I could have just done it myself. It would have been faster and easier, but I kept the end goal in mind. I was raising men, not boys, and I was more concerned with their character than their comfort. My adult sons are now married, and they can cook, clean, manage their finances, and are ideal employees. They thank me now for requiring them to accept responsibility.

Unfortunately, many adults have never learned to "carry their load." This spills over into marriage, as these people expect their spouse and others to do what they never had to do themselves and often marry people who will perpetuate this codependency.

In the story of Nancy's son, the issue was not capacity but willingness. This young man was able but not willing to make changes. He had no interest or motivation in carrying his load. Why should he carry it when Mom was willing to do so?

What burden do you carry because someone in your life isn't willing to step up and carry it themselves? Maybe it's time you set that burden down and let your friend or loved one experience the consequences of not carrying their load. Expect some pushback and be okay with that. You have options if you are willing to exercise them. Emily had the option of telling her husband she could do his books or attend car shows, but not both. Emily had the option to tell her husband that she was unable to care for her mother-in-law at this time. Emily's opinions and choices were equal to that of her husband, but she did not see this as true.

Lorraine, an accomplished accountant, came in to see me for help with her depression. She told me that she and her husband had been married for 30 years and although not physically abusive he had become increasingly verbally abusive with her. It had gone on for years but was getting progressively worse. I asked her why she didn't stand up to him and insist on counseling. She told me she tried, but he just ignored her and kept up with the abuse and refused to go to counseling. I asked her if he had self-control with their neighbors and friends, and she admitted he did. Reminding her and encouraging her of her identity and accomplishments, I advised her to go to her husband and calmly tell him how his words made her feel, and that she expected him to treat her with respect, just as she would with him. If he could not do that, she intended to leave the house every time he was abusive and would come back when he calmed down and could treat her respectfully. If he started it again, she was to turn around and march right out of the house and stay away longer. She told me that it wouldn't work, but I encouraged her to try. I saw her a few months later, and she had implemented the plan. Her husband was stunned when she walked out of the house the first time. She came back an hour later and he started right back in. She turned herself around and left for two hours. He ignored her when she returned the second time. Lorraine went on as if nothing had happened. The next day it happened again, and she turned around as soon as the tirade started and left for an hour. This happened a few more times (he was still testing her lock), but Lorraine was persistent and her husband began to treat her more respectfully. Over the next six months, he agreed to counseling at her insistence and the marriage improved.

Lorraine's husband did not treat her with respect because she had not required this from him. Her boundary had been trampled for quite some time with no consequences. It took several months of her closing this door on him repeatedly for him to figure out she was serious. This caused him to begin to see her in a different light, and his attitude changed. The key was her consistency and follow-through.

If there is any physical abuse between you and a spouse or other family member, you must leave or make them leave. Abuse tends to escalate, and boundaries can become so trampled that your life may be at risk. Getting the other person to stop is out of your control and will have to come from another authority.

Allowing family or friends to chronically abuse resources or emotions because they are unwilling to make changes is just plain foolish, no matter the pressure or guilt they try to apply. Remember, no one can make you feel guilty unless you let them. We do have the ability and authority to say no to misplaced guilt. There are people who will drain you dry financially and emotionally, and neither one of you will have anything to show for it in the end.

Proverbs states that hunger drives a man to work (see Prov. 16:26). There are some people who will not work unless they experience tremendous need. As long as someone else is willing to provide for their needs, they have no drive to fend for themselves. There are others who will verbally abuse and manipulate you if clear boundaries are not enforced. We really can't criticize them for their behavior if we're willing to drop the boundary. The truth is you can't have a bully unless you have a victim. Whose fault is it really?

So what does love look like in these types of situations? Love always looks like something. Love is not a feeling or something you say. Love isn't lazy, and love isn't motivated by fear or guilt. Love is an action that looks like something. Love is the mother who gets up at all hours of the night to care for a fussy baby. Love is the husband who works all day and spends his off hours playing with his kids when he'd rather watch a football game. Love is the mother who takes her protesting child in for immunizations or dental work. Love is the father who refuses to pay for his son to be on the school ski team because he declined to keep the required 3.0 grade average for that privilege. Love doesn't necessarily look pretty or even feel good, and love is willing to be uncomfortable because love keeps the end goal in mind. This is the reason Jesus was able to endure the cross for the joy set before Him. Jesus didn't enjoy the cross; He endured it because He loved us. Love looks like something.

If you are dealing with a loved one who is taking advantage of your resources, go to them and tell them you love them and you believe in them. Describe your boundary matter-of-factly, setting specific expectations (deadlines for getting a job, counseling, paying rent, moving out, etc.). In some cases, a written contract is necessary to avoid hearing, "You never said…!" This tells your loved one that you are no longer willing to carry their load, and you have set it down. Now the burden shifts to your loved one, and it becomes their decision whether or not they are going to pick their burden up. It's important to remember that your loved one has a free will, and their decision may not be your decision. They may not choose to get a job, so by default they've *chosen* the consequences you outlined. You may not like it, but you need to respect their decision because this is a boundary you don't have the right to cross either. What they do with their burden is their choice alone. On the other hand, you've also set a boundary that your loved one does not have the right to cross. Your boundary was a job by a certain date or they had to move out. They can't have it both ways unless you allow it.

It is so important to send a message to your loved one that you respect them and you believe they are competent. When we continually rescue and "take care" of our loved ones we are inadvertently sending a message that we think they can't make it on their own. We may not say it with words, but our actions tell them so. This will be a message that needs to be reiterated over and over again, particularly if the "helping" has gone on for a long time. Your loved one is used to walking through the closed door and taking your stuff because the door was never locked. Once the lock has been placed on the door, expect some rattling and banging. It's important to remind your loved one that just as you respect their choices, they must respect yours. Old habits die hard, so expect resistance and be prepared. Don't open the door, and if need be reinforce the lock. Remember, if you are feeling guilty, there is a good chance you are being manipulated. And if you are being manipulated, it's only because you are allowing it to happen. Keep the end goal in mind, not the conflict in front of you.

Jesus tells the story of a loving father and a wayward son, in which a perfect display of loving boundaries are described. Did you notice that when the son wants to take his inheritance early, the father does not try to stop him? The father respects this boundary. I know I'd have a hard time not trying to talk my son out of such a foolish decision! The father doesn't chase or nag his son about his debauched lifestyle. He doesn't pay his bills, buy him food, or give him rent money. The father doesn't even go out to look for his son. This is because his son is an adult, and the father respects the decision his son has made. It is only when his son is willing to make changes and returns home prepared to work that we see a joyous father blessing his son with his love and resources. If the father had tried to coax or rescue his son, would he have repented? I don't think so. This decision was something the son had to figure out on his own and choose. He came to this decision quickest by reaping the full effect of his choices. I'm sure the father had sleepless nights wondering if his son was hungry, cold, or homeless. But the father had placed his son in God's care, and he trusted God to bring about the needed change in his son. Ultimately, letting go and trusting God is the core issue that people struggle with. The lie is: *I must take responsibility for my loved one because I don't trust that God will do so, and I don't want to feel guilty if it doesn't turn out well.* This begs the question, *Why don't we trust God? What is the source of our unbelief?*

In over 26 years of practice and numerous patient interactions, I've discovered that deep down inside, many people truly don't believe that God is *always* good. That God is good is just a theory. People may say it's true, but their actions belie their words. There is a part of us that believes God is a punisher, and we know we don't *deserve* His love or goodness *always*. Past experiences of having bad things happen to us—such as the death of a loved one, abuse, betrayal, etc.—can cause us to withhold our complete trust in the One who is most trustworthy of all. This is the One who loves us beyond compare, who will not give us a stone if we ask for food, who knows the number of hairs on our head, who leaves the ninety-nine for the one, and who took our sins upon Himself as well as our punishment. That we cannot fully trust Him is incomprehensible when Paul writes:

> *That Christ may dwell in your hearts through faith; that you, being rooted and grounded in love, may be able to comprehend with all the saints what is the width and length and depth and height—to know the love of Christ which passes knowledge* (Ephesians 3:17-19 NKJV).

We do not trust because we do not understand who we are in Christ, and we are not rooted and grounded in love. We believe a lie, and this opens the door to fear.

There is no fear in love. But perfect love drives out fear, because fear has to do with punishment (1 John 4:18).

Many do not understand that we are no longer sinners but saints, joint heirs with Christ. Not because of what we've done, but because of what Christ has done for us.

It is by grace you have been saved. And God raised us up with Christ and seated us with him in the heavenly realms in Christ Jesus (Ephesians 2:5-6).

This means now, not some future time in glory. I may sin, but it now goes against my nature to do so. When I was baptized with Him, I was given a new nature, and the Holy Spirit now dwells in me. It is now my nature to be a saint—righteous and holy just like the Holy Spirit inside me. What Jesus Christ did for me on the cross was enough to not only cover my past but to allow me to live in holiness now. When I do go against my nature and sin, His blood covers me both now and in the future.

For we know that our old self was crucified with him…that we should no longer be slaves to sin—because anyone who has died has been set free from sin (Romans 6:6-7).

Did you know that when the Father looks at you, He sees Jesus? His love is perfect and is not contaminated with even the slightest bit of punishment. We know how much we love our own children. How could we possibly think our love could ever exceed the Father's love? When we understand how much we are loved, then we can trust the One who orders our very steps with everything.

People often confuse discipline with punishment, for God disciplines those He loves. But discipline is different from punishment. Discipline is actually a demonstration of God's love and His mercy to correct me away from error. I love to garden, and I have nearly 100 roses in my backyard. In the winter time, I spend many hours pruning each of those plants by hand, cutting away any diseased, weak, or old growth. My pruned roses look stark and pathetic compared to their previous state. My pruning is a correction of their growth, and it's done out of a desire to get a healthy plant with beautiful roses. I don't just whack haphazardly at the roses to punish them. I carefully select which canes stay and which go. The benefits of my pruning are seen a few months later in the spring, with lovely roses and healthy plants. This is how our loving Father disciplines us. His cuts may be painful, and we may feel exposed, but we are not being punished. Time will show that the correction was strategic, and our lives are healthier and more productive because of His loving discipline.

I have learned to welcome the discipline of God because I am not a fool. Proverbs is a good read if you want to know more about the wise man who seeks correction and the fool who declines. I would much rather receive the discipline of God than the punishment of man. I have discovered that even when discipline is painful, it's still full of love and the entire process is meant for my good. Never has God turned His face from me, never has He punished me (even though I clearly deserved it), never has He been anything but faithful (even though it didn't look like it at first), and never has He been anything but *always* good. God's punishment is reserved for demonic entities, not His children.

The result of our inability to trust God is a belief in the lie that *we should be a god to others.* If I don't believe that God will rescue my loved one who is entrenched in a destructive lifestyle, then chances are I will try to "help" them, thus keeping them from reaching their bottom where repentance occurs and God can reach them. My "help" in essence becomes a hindrance to God's plan.

When we try to be a god to others we tie God's hands and prevent the very thing we want to see happen. It's time to put these unsanctified burdens down and let the real God take over. In the process, we need to remember that God has His own way of doing things and His ways are not our ways. We need to trust in the fact that He is always good and has our best interests at heart, even if things look bleak or get worse before they get better. I suspect that God is waiting for a lot of people to get out the way, so He can do what He does best. Instead of being a god, our role is to partner with God through prayer and respect the decisions of our loved ones even when we don't agree. We can love them when they are unlovely and allow God to work in their lives unhindered by us. It is time to bring our burdens to God in prayer and allow Him to carry them as well as refuse to take on false guilt for the choices of others.

ACTION POINTS

1. What has the Father asked you to do with what He's given you? Where has He asked you to focus your time, energies, and resources?

2. Do you feel that you are a victim and that others are controlling you? What are the doors you haven't locked?

3. Where or who are you looking to for acceptance? Be honest and ask the Lord to forgive you if it's really not Him.

4. What burdens are you carrying that don't belong to you? Spend some time in prayer and ask the Lord to show you. In your mind visualize yourself setting that burden in front of God and ask the Lord to forgive you for trying to be god in that situation.

5. Are you feeling guilty for setting boundaries or for the actions of others? Ask the Lord to show you the lie, because the guilt is false. As you recognize the lie and the false guilt, visualize yourself throwing it in the trash where it belongs. The lie will return and try to gain entry. So when it comes knocking, keep your door locked. If you realize you let it in, then stick it back in the trash again. If you do this enough, it will quit knocking.

Chapter 8

Nourish Your Mind

"You cannot have a positive life and a negative mind."
—JOYCE MEYER

Now that we've reviewed the importance of establishing healthy boundaries, let's discuss practical ways to nourish the mind. In earlier chapters, the importance of nutrition, exercise, and sleep to mental health was reviewed. In the same way that physical health comes from eating good foods, avoiding junk food, and exercising, good mental health comes from consuming healthy information and exercising the brain by meditating on kind thoughts.

There are numerous patients in my medical practice who struggle with the triad of elevated blood pressure, high cholesterol, and diabetes. These patients have a condition called dysmetabolic syndrome and are in the highest risk category for dying prematurely from heart disease. Although other risk factors for heart disease may be present, the primary cause of this syndrome is obesity. For many patients, losing weight will normalize blood pressure, cholesterol, and blood sugar. If I can get my patients to eat the appropriate amount of the right food and exercise so that they can make changes in their metabolism and vascular system, their disease state resolves or at least substantially improves. This is incredible, and patients are delighted when they can take away three or four medications just by taking control of what they eat and by exercising.

This analogy holds true for mental health as well. When we feed our mind negative, angry, fearful, accusatory information, our thoughts, feelings, and words reflect what we consume. As junk food leads to obesity, consuming negative material leads to fear, anxiety, hopelessness, anger, and depression. You are what you consume, both physically and mentally. This is why Paul wrote:

> *Rejoice in the Lord always. I will say it again: Rejoice! Let your gentleness be evident to all. The Lord is near. Do not be anxious about anything, but in every situation, by prayer and petition, with thanksgiving, present your requests to God. And the peace of God, which transcends all understanding, will guard your hearts and your minds in Christ Jesus. Finally, brothers and sisters, whatever is true, whatever is noble, whatever is right, whatever is pure, whatever is lovely, whatever is admirable—if anything is excellent or praiseworthy—think about such things...and the God of peace will be with you* (Philippians 4:4-9).

This passage of Scripture is powerful and foundational for every follower of Jesus for several reasons. First, we are commanded to rejoice in the Lord always (no matter our circumstances). Praise resets our focus away from our circumstances to the one who holds the world in His hands. In other words, praise renews our mind.

If that isn't challenging enough, we are commanded to abstain from *all* anxiety. There is no wiggle room here. Anxiety is the result of fear, and it's not allowed under any circumstances. Instead, we are told to present our requests and thanksgivings to God, with the promise that the peace of God (peace that surpasses the facts of our circumstances) will guard our hearts and our minds in Christ Jesus. Think about that for a minute. Paul is telling us that when we turn our attention away from our circumstances and take on an attitude of thanksgiving as we present our prayers to God, the Father gives us a gift of peace that protects our mind. We don't have to understand or know the plans of the Father to have peace.

God's Purpose for Us Is Peace, Not Understanding

We humans want to "understand" why we are going through hard times and we want to see the path that shows us the way out. Understanding helps us feel in control. I know this both from personal experience and from talking to hundreds of patients who have gone through very difficult trials. I hate having to tell patients that their lab or x-ray results are abnormal, and I need them to go back for additional testing. I know I will be inundated with all sorts of questions about potential diagnoses, which I am unable to answer. The process of waiting for additional test results is nerve-wracking. People want to understand right now, and that's not always possible.

We do this with God as well. We want answers. Obviously, God has the answers, but I've often discovered that He declines to give them to me! He is far more interested in my level of faith and trust than in my emotional comfort.

No matter where we are in life, we come back to that essential element in our relationship with God—faith. This is why it's called the *"walk of faith."* When He returns, he's looking for "faith" on the earth. Do you trust Him? At times I think I do, until I discover another area that, when tested, produces anxiety instead of faith. It's a process that continually polishes my edges and at times is like a furnace that purifies me by removing the dross. It's not fun, but the end result is beautiful.

The last portion of the passage above tells us what to *feed* our mind. Are you reading, listening to, and thinking about things that are true, noble, right, pure, lovely, admirable, excellent, and praiseworthy? What would your life be like if you avoided television, radio, Internet, newspapers, magazines, books, and in some cases people who did not give you information that meets the criteria listed above?

Paul wrote this in an era when there was no Internet, newspaper, computer, radio, or television news. In Roman times, people obtained their news from a neighbor or perhaps the marketplace. News would have primarily been local or regional. Paul understood that we have a penchant for bad news. In fact, humans are hard-wired to look for threats for survival purposes. The portion of our brain that evaluates potential risks is in the amygdala, an area that initiates our flight-fight response to danger. The news media in modern times understands this quite well, which is why the majority of news is negative. Negative or scary news captures our attention, and because media is designed to make a profit, news stories follow suit. We are surrounded by news 24/7, and to the extent we can we need to control the amount and type of information we allow our minds to absorb.

If you find yourself feeling angry, helpless, or sad after listening to media, then limit your exposure. Most of the time there is very little you can do to change the situation of the news story being reported, particularly national or international issues. Yes, you should be informed, but it's not healthy to dwell on something out of your control. This boundary is different for each individual. Personally, I read my local newspaper because I feel responsible for my community, and there is often a way for me to get involved to make things better. Internet news is also a way to control the quantity and type of news being reported and is a good way to avoid hearing the same negative story repeatedly. Being selective on the quality and quantity of the news to which you expose your mind is necessary and wise. On a side note, use your feelings as a gauge to let you know if you are nourishing your mind. The result of nourishing your mind is joy, peace, hope, and anticipation for the future. If your primary source of information makes you feel angry, sad, or helpless, then change it or turn it off.

So what about good news? It's harder to find, but it is out there. There are numerous websites devoted to news that is encouraging and inspiring. If you read or listen to the regular news, make sure you counter it with a reality check. There are lots of good things happening in the world around us, and we need to focus our attention on things that make us feel hopeful and happy.

If I am honest, the majority of people I know are happily married and avoid shoplifting, burglary, murder, drug dealing, violence, and all of the other negative social behaviors that fill the airways. Probably most of the people you know are doing good things to take care of their loved ones and are trying to make their communities better. The reality is that we are surrounded by good things if we look for them. I have friends who spend their time helping people out of poverty, clean up our river trails, house international students, and volunteer with numerous community organizations. I know people with lots of positive stories, and these are the people who inspire me to make the world a better place. These are the stories that need to nourish my mind and are the things that are noble, pure, lovely, and praiseworthy.

Unfortunately, our culture trains us from infancy to look for negative things so that we can correct them. This is not necessarily bad, but when taken out of context it becomes distorted. You may get 98 percent correct on a test, but instead of rejoicing on how much was right, you ruminate over the one problem you missed. I have found this obsession with looking for what's wrong to be common in many of my depressed and anxious patients.

Angela, a 39-year-old professional woman, is a manager at a local marketing agency. She has a great husband, good health, and a good job. When I asked her why she was anxious and depressed, she pointed to her perceived failures at work and marriage. As I questioned her about job performance ratings and her husband's view of the relationship, I found that Angela had a distorted view of herself. Like the person who scores 98 percent on the test above and ruminates on the 2 percent missed, Angela had focused all of her attention on small areas that were not perfect. In reality, her husband adored her, and she was highly regarded by her boss and peers. She just couldn't see it because she was staring at small flaws. I don't know about you, but I've never found this to be helpful. What would Angela's world look like if she focused on all of the positive things in her life?

Did you know that you find what you are looking for? So why not spend your time looking for good things like Paul advised us to do? I had a revelation of this principle just recently. It was springtime, and as gardening is a huge hobby of mine I was out in the garden cleaning up dead growth. In my yard are roses and a large flowering perennial bed that is stunning in the spring. This particular day I was working in an area that had quite a bit of dead growth that needed to be pruned, and debris I was removing from border rocks. As I picked up the rocks, creepy crawly things scurried away. I worked in this little area for quite some time, and I realized that if this is all I ever saw or spoke about in my garden, the people I talked to would think my garden was quite ugly. Once I walked away from this area and looked up to see the beauty of the entire garden my whole perspective changed. Yes, there are creepy, dead things in my garden, but that is not the "truth" of my garden. You find what you are looking for, so why not look for things that are good, right, lovely, pure, excellent, admirable, and praiseworthy? Your brain will be much happier for it!

If you start looking for good news, you will find it everywhere. The best place to start is the word of God. God's word will nourish your mind like no other, so make sure you spend time there every day. There are numerous excellent devotionals that are widely available as well. One of my favorites is *Blessing Your Spirit* by S. Gunter and A. Burk.

There are some great websites that focus on good news. Both sunny-skyz.com and goodnewsnetwork.org are excellent sources of inspirational news. Inspirational stories and books abound. Check out the recommended reading lists of inspirational books on Amazon and Goodreads. There is enough material in the world around you to last a lifetime if you look.

There is one additional point I'd like to reiterate, and that is the importance of keeping truths in perspective. It is critical that we look at the entire picture, just like my garden story above. When truths are taken out of perspective or context, they become untrue. We are bombarded daily by media, both secular and religious, that shout, *"Things are getting worse, our planet is failing, we are going to hell in a hand-basket, and you should be afraid."* This is the message in the airwaves, and it influences how we think if we don't fill our mind with the *whole* truth.

Are things getting worse? Most people would probably say yes, but is that true? As a medical professional, I can tell you that things are getting better. Did you know that life expectancy up until 1900 was about 30 years? As of 2010 it had risen to 68 years. Currently in the United Statess, life expectancy is 79 years and continues to go up. Aren't you glad you're not living in 1900? Infant mortality alone has dropped 80 percent in the past 50 years. These are huge advances. We think nothing of going to see our doctor to get a prescription for an antibiotic to treat an infection that would have killed us 100 years ago, not to mention the advances we've made in treating diabetes, cancer, heart disease, and hypertension, diseases we had no treatment for until the last century.

I know that I am quite grateful for air conditioning, electricity, modern transportation, computer technology, and other scientific advances that make my life more comfortable and safe. Certainly, as a woman I am grateful I live in a time when I can vote, become educated, choose a career, and am less likely to suffer abuse by the men in my world. *It's Getting Better All the Time: 100 Greatest Trends of the Last 100 Years* by S. Moore and J. Simon is a great read of the advances made in health, nutrition, income, education, safety, etc., demonstrating that many things are getting better, not worse.

Our God is neither surprised nor afraid of earth's condition. Jesus knew that the cross was in His future from the foundation of the world. His Kingdom has come, and it is increasing in nature, not decreasing.

> *For to us a child is born, to us a son is given, and the government will be on his shoulders. And he will be called Wonderful Counselor, Mighty God, Everlasting Father, Prince of Peace. Of the greatness of his government and peace there will be no end. He will reign on David's throne and over his kingdom, establishing and upholding it with justice and righteousness from that time on and forever. The zeal of the Lord Almighty will accomplish this* (Isaiah 9:6-7).

Your purpose on this earth is to extend the Kingdom of God wherever you place your feet. Whether it's in your home, church, marketplace, or faraway lands, you are part of an ever-increasing Kingdom of peace. No matter the trials you may face, you are and you will be victorious. To this end, nourish your mind in the direction that fulfills your destiny. Your brain will be happier for it.

ACTION POINTS

1. What are the current sources of nourishment for your mind?

_____

_____

_____

_____

2. Read Philippians 4:4-9.   Do these sources meet the criteria listed by Paul to think about, and do these sources of nourishment make you feel encouraged or discouraged?

_____

_____

_____

_____

3. If you are not doing so, spend some time daily nourishing your mind on the word of God. Use feelings as a gauge. Once you start to feel encouraged, joyful, and full of hope, you know the nourishment has kicked in.

4. Check out goodnewsnetwork.org and sunnyskyz.com. Focus your attention on what is right and good in the world around you. Write out some good things and meditate on them.

_____

_____

_____

_____

5. Does what you read, watch, or think about inspire you to fulfill your destiny? If not, then what do you need to get rid of, and what do you need to add to give your mind the proper nourishment?

_____

_____

_____

_____

_____

Chapter 9

Stay in the Now and Keep Kind Thoughts

"Be present in all things and thankful for all things."
—Maya Angelou

To live in the present and keep our thoughts kind is an extension of the previous chapter on nourishing our mind. If I could get my patients to live in the present, much of their anxiety and depression would dissipate. The mistakes and failures of the past and the uncertainty of tomorrow can create sad and worrisome thoughts for all of us. However, each day is a gift, and in reality we can only live in the moment we are in.

Grant is a patient I've seen for major depressive disorder for many years. He was emotionally neglected as a child and has regrets about his past mistakes of substance abuse and immorality. He ruminates on the failures and injustices of the past. Although Grant has a wonderful wife and family, a successful career, and the respect of his peers, his past keeps him from enjoying the present and causes him to view his future with dread.

When we ruminate over past mistakes and injustices, beating ourselves and others over what should have happened, we needlessly waste time and emotional energy on something that cannot be changed. Learning from our past is useful, but wallowing is both ineffective and unhealthy. Forgiving ourselves and others is the key to letting go of the past. If you feel haunted by the past, then reread the earlier chapter on "Forgiveness." Our loving Father does not remind us of past failures as He is perfect love and His forgiveness is complete. If God does not punish us, who are we to punish ourselves or others for past mistakes?

> *There is no fear in love. But perfect love drives out fear, because fear has to do with punishment. The one who fears is not made perfect in love* (1 John 4:18).

You, beloved, are made perfect in love. God's overwhelming, immeasurable, unfathomable, eternal love rewrites your past and gives you strength in the present and security in the future. God's love is more than enough for every circumstance you face.

Living in the past is futile, and so is worrying about the future. Jesus said:

> *Therefore do not worry about tomorrow, for tomorrow will worry about itself. Each day has enough trouble of its own* (Matthew 6:34).

Most of my anxious patients live in a future that will never take place. They create all kinds of scary "What if?" scenarios out of thin air. These threatening thoughts are a waste of time that taxes their brain and emotions, leaving them unable to enjoy the beauty in the present.

As I walked into the exam room, I noticed that Lisa was a bundle of nerves. She requested a sleeping medication because her circling, worrisome thoughts were keeping her from falling asleep. When I asked her why she was worried, she told me that her employer had been bought out by another company. She didn't know if this was good or bad. She had not been told that her job would change, but she had already assumed that she would be laid off. She could see that this would cause her to lose her mortgage and then she would have to move. None of these things had occurred, but she was worried they might. Lisa's brain could not differentiate between real and imagined threats. Her worrisome thoughts were not helpful to her current situation as they were not able to save her job or pay her bills. Her thoughts only made her ill. I asked Lisa about another potential scenario. What if the new owner had more money to invest in the company and this created a positive opportunity for her advancement? She stared at me blankly. This thought had not crossed her mind. Both scenarios were possible, so why waste time and emotional energy on something that may not take place?

There is nothing wrong with planning for the future. In fact, it's wise to do so. But worrying about the future is unhealthy and robs us of joy in the present. Plan for the future but live in the now. If you tend to be a worrier, turn that focus into goal-setting. If you find yourself worrying about some potential future disaster, turn your focus to what you want to become. This helps turn fearful thoughts back to a reality that you can do something about.

So how do you live in the present? Jesus gave us a great model for living in the moment. Although Jesus knew that He only had three years of active ministry time before His death, He never appeared hurried or anxious. We don't see Him rushing from one city to another or ignoring the needs of the people around Him. Jesus was fully present. He spent time blessing children. I know it sounds sweet, but I doubt most ministers could make time in their busy schedules to enjoy sitting and blessing children, particularly if they knew that their ministry time was limited to three years. Jesus lived fully present as He walked through towns talking to lepers, the woman at the well, and the centurion soldier. He was so at peace in the present that He could sleep on a boat in a storm, eat with a tax collector, attend a wedding, and stop to talk to a woman who just touched His robe. We don't see Jesus ruminating about the past or regretting missed opportunities and failures. Of course, Jesus was sinless and made no mistakes, but what about those closest to Him? The New Testament is rife with some of the bumbles and failures of the disciples. Jesus corrects them in the present but moves on. Never does He remind His disciples of their past mistakes. Oh, if we could just leave our mistakes in the past where they belong!

Each day is new and fresh, full of grace to accomplish all that is needed. I wonder how much joy and conversation with God we miss because we are not mindful of the present. He wants to do something with us now, but our mind is reliving past failures, worrying about the future, or just thinking about the things we need to get done.

How often do you stop in your busy day to just breathe deeply, listen to the sounds, and smell the scents around you? I am preaching to myself here as this is an area where I could improve. Although I'm not one to ruminate in the past or worry about the future, I tend to be thinking of the next thing I need to do. This pursuit often robs me of daily gifts meant to bless me and lower my level of stress. When I take the time in the morning to go out on the patio and spend some time with a hot, fragrant cup of coffee, attune my ear to the birds, feel the cool breeze across my face, and focus my attention on the scent of the roses, I feel my blood pressure drop and a sense of peace fill my soul and spirit. Living in the present is a way to appreciate not only God's creation and gifts but His very presence.

If you can just stop for a few minutes throughout the day to focus on the present, you can change your mood and lower your stress. There are several very simple things you can do to live in the now. First, take just one task and focus your attention on what you are doing. If you are cleaning, think about how the rag feels in your hand, the sensation of wiping away dust and the beauty of the surface you've just cleaned. If your mind tries to wander to other things, bring it back to focus on the task at hand. Multitasking is the enemy to mindfulness. I must confess, I am a skilled multitasker, and when I focus on just one task I feel guilty. However, when I can just enjoy the mindfulness of cleaning or working in the yard, I feel relaxed, and the stress melts away. This is because I am living in the moment.

Take just a couple of minutes at work to shut your eyes, breathe deeply, and simply think about the moment. What do you hear, smell, sense? This type of activity is soothing to the brain and will actually lower blood pressure. Taking timeouts like this is a good way to listen to what the Holy Spirit is saying to you and to meditate on all that you are thankful for.

KIND THOUGHTS

The definition of kindness is to demonstrate "a gentle nature and a desire to help others; wanting and liking to do good things and to bring happiness to others."[1] Kindness is a fruit of the spirit that is both gentle and powerful. We all want to be around people who are kind, and we tend to shun those who are unkind. One of the things we teach our children is to be kind to others, as most cultures value kindness. In spite of this we are often very unkind to ourselves.

Did you know that you talk to yourself constantly in your head? It's called self-talk or self-dialogue, and we all do it. The very nature of that talk directs and shapes mood like a riverbed directs water. Water follows gravity without choice. If the riverbed is altered, water will follow. So it is with our mood. Our mood is like the water, flowing through a riverbed formed by our thoughts. Unkind self-talk causes us to feel sad, hopeless, angry, overwhelmed, and fearful. There are no other results possible.

Some of the things we say to ourselves we would never say to another. Can you imagine telling your friend the following?

"You never do anything right."

"You are a total failure."

"You are so ugly."

"You will never be a success."

"No one will ever marry you."

These statements are not only abusive; they are untrue. God does not speak like this to us, and even though we may have had parents who spoke unkind words to us we must model the kindness found in our perfect Father.

I have discovered that God is very kind to me. His words and actions toward me are always encouraging and loving. Even in discipline I feel His kindness and love. Never does He speak to me in a demeaning, harsh, or critical manner. Oh, if I could be as kind to myself and others as God is to me, my life would look much different.

Candace is a new patient in our practice. She is 35 years old, married, and has two children whom she home schools. Her husband works out of town all week, so she bears most of the household and child-rearing responsibilities. She came into the office on her last visit in tears, saying that she felt overwhelmed. Unable to keep up with all of her household chores made her feel like a failure. She was also frustrated with the ten pounds she had been unable to take off after her last pregnancy, and this made her feel like an "obese slug." Although she went to bed at eleven P.M. and got up at six A.M., she was quite angry with herself for not getting up 30 minutes earlier to exercise. She spent ten minutes venting her failures, and not once did she mention the positive things she was doing to raise and educate her family, primarily alone. This woman was tormented by her negative self-talk. How could she possibly feel peace and joy?

I redirected Candace to tell me all of the positive things about herself. Her expression told me that she thought this was a dumb idea, but she reluctantly agreed. It took her several moments to come up with anything. I gently pointed out that she had healthy, happy children who were doing well in school, so she was obviously a good teacher. So, "What else are you doing right?" I asked her. She told me that she took nutrition very seriously, and she carefully shopped and prepared healthy meals, allowing no junk food in the home. This admission reminded her of the volunteer time she spent coaching her daughter's softball team, as well as the care she was giving to an ill parent. As she recounted her kindness to her family and others, her countenance changed and a smile appeared.

In reality, Candace was an amazing woman, but her internal dialogue not only focused her thoughts on her perceived failures but magnified them out of proportion to reality. Being ten pounds overweight is nowhere close to being an "obese slug." Her inability to see that she was doing an amazing job of parenting was obscured by the deluge of unkind self-talk that magnified her flaws.

So why are we so unkind to ourselves? I suspect we are unkind to ourselves in the mistaken belief that recognition of our good qualities is prideful and that reminding ourselves of our deficiencies will somehow punish us into doing better. Neither of these things is true. Our self-talk needs to be based on truth. We need to admit both our strengths and weaknesses in a way that is helpful. When we acknowledge our generosity and what our compassion brings to others, we feel gratified. Not only is this truthful, but it propels us to increase our kindness toward others. When we acknowledge our weaknesses, our self-talk should be honest. Instead of telling ourselves we are a complete failure, we tell ourselves we will do better next time in that particular area.

When a teacher asked Jesus which commandment was the greatest given, Jesus answered:

> *"Love the Lord your God with all your heart and with all your soul and with all your mind." ...And the second is like it: "Love your neighbor as yourself." All of the Law and the Prophets hang on these two commandments* (Matthew 22:37-40).

I find it interesting that Jesus linked these two commandments together. All other laws given to us are summed up in these foundational commandments. If we can do these two things there is no need for other rules. When we love God unreservedly, with every part of our being, we then see how much we are loved. If I am loved so greatly by Him, then I must value and take care of my body, my mind, and my spirit, and I must love my neighbor likewise. How can we love others well when we do not love ourselves? The people I encounter who love others the best are those who respect and love themselves. They know that they are not perfect, but they have turned their thoughts to that which is true, noble, right, pure, lovely, admirable, and excellent in both themselves and others. This is the kind of self-talk we all need to utilize

I will end this chapter by reiterating the kindness found in God. The absolute loving kindness of our Father is a constant source of comfort and should draw us like a beacon to His presence. The more time we spend with Him, the more kindness we find. He loves us unreservedly and desires our companionship. We can talk to Him about little things and big things, and it's all of interest to Him. When I look for His kindness, I see it everywhere, and it brings great comfort and delight. If He values me this much, how can I treat myself or others unkindly?

ACTION POINTS

1. If you reflect upon your thought life, where do you spend most of your time—past, present, future?

   _____

   _____

   _____

   _____

   _____

2. If you struggle with living in the present, how does living in the past or future affect your mood?

   _____

   _____

   _____

   _____

   _____

3. Ask the Father to show you what failures or injuries you need to forgive and leave in the past. Ask also what fears you need to repent of that take your thoughts to a worrisome future.

   _____

   _____

   _____

   _____

   _____

4. As you think about your daily routine, ask the Lord to show you how and where you can take a few minutes to focus on shutting everything off and focus on the present.

   _____

   _____

5. Meditate:

> *Praise the Lord, my soul, and forget not all his benefits—who forgives all your sins and heals all your diseases, who redeems your life from the pit and crowns you with love and compassion, who satisfies your desires with good things so that your youth is renewed like the eagle's* (Psalm 103:2-5).

> *Many, Lord my God, are the wonders you have done, the things you planned for us. None can compare with you; were I to speak and tell of your deeds, they would be too many to declare* (Psalm 40:5).

6. Does your self-talk primarily circle around your failures and deficiencies? If so, what does God say about you? What are you good at and how do you serve others?

7. If your self-talk is abusive, it needs to change. Practice writing out how you could truthfully reword your self-talk so that it becomes constructive instead of condemning. An example might be instead of "I am a complete failure," change to "Although I don't know how to do that yet, I will learn."

NOTE

1. Merriam-Webster Dictionary, s.v. "Kind," http://www.merriam-webster
    .com/dictionary/kind.

Chapter 10

Identity: Who Are You?

*"Your identity is your most valuable
possession. Protect it."*
—ELASTIGIRL, *The Incredibles*

We now move from psychological to spiritual keys that help us stay rooted in joy. Understanding your identity, or who you are, is elemental to a lifestyle of peace and joy. Anxiety and depression are common in those who don't know who they are or whose they are. When we get a glimpse of the vastness of God's love for us, everything changes internally. Personally, my identity in Christ has been a journey of revelation. I know more now than I did as a young woman, but there is still so much more to discover about Him. The more I spend time with Him, the more I know Him and the more He knows me. An exchange occurs, and I become more like my heavenly Father. As He is not worried but full of faith and love, I find that this mindset becomes available to me. Understanding who I am drives out fear and gives me the courage to pursue big dreams.

So who am I? In the natural, if someone asks me that question I tell them my name, to whom I'm married, and my profession. However, on a deeper level I think of myself from the perspective of a family line. I am a daughter, granddaughter, wife, sister, mother, and grandmother with a lineage I can trace back several hundred years. My family history is a part of my natural identity, but there is a significantly greater spiritual history that shapes how I view myself in both time and space. As a little girl, when I told Jesus I wanted Him to be my Lord, my identity immediately changed.

He predestined us for adoption to sonship through Jesus Christ,
in accordance with his pleasure and will (Ephesians 1:5).

I did not realize it then, but I had been adopted by the King of kings. I had become a royal daughter. My papa is a king, so this made me a princess. Unfortunately, I did not grasp the fullness of this truth until many years later. I did not think of myself as a princess, nor did I act like one.

Yet to all who did receive him, to those who believed in his
name, he gave the right to become children of God (John 1:12).

In the natural, if you are a son or daughter of royalty, you are trained in the ways of royalty from infancy. There is an expectation that you will work hard, study, and behave in a way that will lead your people honorably. Your name is known by everyone, and your behavior is ever before the public eye. Children of royals are raised differently than the children of common people. They are trained with the understanding that the Kingdom is far more important than their personal desires and that others depend on them to make good decisions.

Royal children not only understand their heritage, but they accept the unusual resources that are available to them. Their name, position, money, and favor opens doors and gives them access to people and opportunities denied to others. If their ruling parents approve, there is very little that can stand in the way of the desires of royal offspring. Royal children do not doubt their identity. Kris Vallotton—the author of *The Supernatural Ways of Royalty,* which I highly recommend—writes about this subject in much greater detail.

We too, as sons and daughters of the King, were chosen by Him and have become a royal priesthood with a purpose.

> *But you are a chosen people, a royal priesthood, a holy nation, God's special possession, that you may declare the praises of him who called you out of darkness into his wonderful light* (1 Peter 2:9).

The problem for many followers of Jesus is that they do not comprehend or accept their spiritual family line. Many theoretically believe they are a son or a daughter of God, but they do not see themselves as favored or as royal, and this is reflected in their behavior. It's as though they live in the village where the king rules, but they live on the outside of the castle with the common people, not from within the ruling castle. God is their king, but not their papa. These royal orphans are fearful and sad simply because they don't understand their lineage. They look at their circumstances through the eyes of a commoner.

I met Kenneth a few years ago when he was 23 years old. He had moved to Redding to attend school and was struggling with anxiety. Kenneth admitted that anxiety and depression had been an intermittent problem for the last seven years. This young man had been raised by a mom who struggled to make ends meet after her husband deserted the family when Kenneth was five years old. His first year of school focused on his identity in Christ, and for Kenneth this brought up some very painful memories.

He struggled to grasp the concepts. While everyone else was rejoicing in their new-found freedom, Kenneth felt like he was drowning.

Who we believe ourselves to be, our identity, sets the course of how we think and behave. If we are limited to an occasional wave at the king when he passes through the village as opposed to being able to gain entrance to his private chambers, what we ask for or expect to receive will be drastically different.

Kenneth lived in the village. God's word did not feel true to him, and he acted accordingly. As Kenneth had never done any counseling, I encouraged him to start there and to incorporate some of the lifestyle recommendations of nutrition, exercise, and sleep discussed in future chapters. I also advised Kenneth to pursue a prayer session with a *Sozo* counselor, which he had not yet done. Six weeks later, I saw him back for follow-up, and Kenneth had made substantial improvement. The anxiety and insomnia had lessened as he began to experience the truth of God's word penetrating his mind. A few months later I saw him in the office for another issue, and I discovered a very joyful young man, brimming with hope and confidence. He told me that God had shown him how much he was loved and that he had a purpose and calling on his life that now felt true. Kenneth had moved from the village to the castle.

Several years ago, a patient of mine, Leah, and her husband, Jake, adopted two little boys aged nine and ten. These two children had been physically abused and had been starved of both love and food since birth. Coming into a household where there was plenty of both did not change their behavior, at least not initially. At meal time, these boys would be the first to grab for the bowls of food. Although there was plenty of food at each meal, the boys hid food in their napkins to take to their room for later. When Leah and Jake affectionately hugged them, the boys stiffened, attempting to avoid all contact. These children expected to be physically hurt and starved because this is what they had experienced from their biological parents. Even though they had been adopted, just as God adopted us, they did not believe in the goodness of their new parents. Until these boys understood that their situation had truly changed and that Leah and Jake could be trusted, they lived with an old identity mindset and their expectations and behaviors reflected their old identity.

Our expectations and behaviors are grounded in our identity.

It took about two years of consistent pursuit by Leah and Jake to gain the trust of these boys and for their behavior to change. The boys have since flourished and are now in college, an amazing testament to Leah and Jake's persistent love.

You can take the king out of the palace, but you can't take the palace out of a king.

A king placed in poor circumstances will still believe himself to be a king and will make decisions based on his identity. Similarly, a poor man placed into a position of authority will still behave like a poor man. Circumstances may change, but identity is internal and does not change easily.

I know many followers of Jesus who have a minimal understanding of who they are in Christ. Their behavior reflects a false identity, and they act like orphans, not adopted and beloved royal children. Instead of living with purpose and joy, secure in their identity, they live with an old poverty mindset. They are unaware of the access they have to their papa and live in fear that what they have will be taken from them.

I doubt the son or daughter of a king worries about what they will wear or if there will be enough food for the week. They believe there will always be enough, and their minds are set on higher purposes. Oh, how I wish we could grasp how much Christ adores, protects, provides, pursues, and lives in us. Our expectations and behaviors would be much different.

The fullness of Christ, who is head over all of creation and every ruling power, lives inside of us. This is a powerful statement, one that I have all too often skipped over because it seemed too extraordinary and unreal. I wonder what would happen in the Body of Christ if followers of Jesus believed that the fullness of Christ (not just a part of Christ) lived inside of them?

> *For in Christ all the fullness of the Deity lives in bodily form, and in Christ you have been brought to fullness. He is the head over every power and authority* (Colossians 2:9-10).

Meredith, a lovely patient of mine for many years, has no grasp of who she is in Christ. The statement above has not penetrated her heart and mind, so it has no effect or benefit for her. She suffers from low self-esteem and has minimal courage. Although Meredith loves God, she does not believe that Christ lives in her and that He adores her. Her lack of identity in Jesus and her expectations of what she can do in Christ cause her to limit her expectations to what she alone can accomplish. Meredith has worked for her current employer for many years with excellent employee reviews but is afraid to ask for a raise. Her poor self-esteem is projected outward, and others treat her in the same way that she perceives herself. At the age of 52 and living her entire life in the church, I would expect Meredith to grasp the power of Christ living inside her. Although Meredith lives in the castle and can knock on the king's door at any hour, she acts as though she lives in the village. When I talk to Meredith about her identity in Christ, she nods in agreement, but I can tell the words do not penetrate her heart.

Do you truly believe you are the daughter or son of a king? Do you live in the castle or the village? Can you knock on the king's private door and expect to gain entrance at any hour? Will your papa move all of his resources to make sure you come into your destiny? If you get into trouble will your papa rescue you? Are you concerned about His Kingdom and your role there or more common things like finances? If you are unable to answer a resounding *yes* to all of these questions, you do not yet know who you are in Christ.

I suspect that the reason many of us do not grasp the fullness and the superiority of our spiritual identity is because we still live from the old mindset of our natural identity. We may have come from broken homes with poor examples of parenting, and we have transferred that warped view of parenting to God. Perhaps our natural parents were absent, distant, critical, abusive, disdainful, self-absorbed, etc. and we view God similarly. We are like the two little boys in the story above who were unable to trust Leah and Jake because of their earlier example of parenting. Maybe we did poorly in school and considered ourselves stupid. Or we don't like our hair, skin, weight, height, etc. and consider ourselves unattractive. Our identity can be anchored in our physical traits and natural skills, which are often unreliable as beauty, health, and skills may not last. Our spiritual identity, however, is permanent, reliable, and true. This is the identity from which we need to think and act.

The question then becomes, how do you take on the reality of your royal identity? First, I want to point out that your identity in Christ is rock solid, and you can't change it. You do have the ability to believe or not believe, but it doesn't change the fact that you were adopted by the king and you are a coheir with Christ. You can choose to live in the castle or the village, but you are still a royal son or daughter. You can knock on the king's chamber door and gain entrance whenever you like, or you can wave periodically from a distance. You can worry about the concerns of commoners, or you can concern yourself with the affairs of your king. These choices are yours alone, and God will not make them for you. Your papa loves you and wants you to choose to believe what he says about you out of faith and trust.

The secret to accepting and living from your true identity is to wash your mind with the word of truth until your spiritual identity feels true to you. In another chapter, we talk about how the word of God is like no other. God's word is alive, and it can divide joint and marrow. When we repeatedly apply His word to our thoughts through meditation, the word changes how we think. The key is to find out what God says about you and live from this truth.

It doesn't matter what your family, teachers, friends, or coworkers have said. What does God say? This is the truth, and this is where you meditate and put your attention, casting down every other thought that is not obedient to the knowledge of Christ.

So who are you in Jesus? First of all, you are a masterpiece with a destiny. Your birth was not an accident, no matter the circumstances. God planned for you and took great delight in you from the beginning of creation. He created you with a destiny for good things. The circumstances of your natural lineage and your conception are irrelevant to Him. If you have an unfortunate natural family line or were born from unplanned or violent circumstances, I want you to wash your mind with this truth until it changes your identity. There is no one else like you. You are an original and God is pleased with you. The cross gave you a new family line.

> *For we are God's masterpiece. He has created us anew in Christ Jesus, so we can do the good things he planned for us long ago* (Ephesians 2:10 NLT).

You are loved for all of eternity. There is nothing you can do that will change God's love for you. There is no place you can go where His love won't find you. Do you love your children? Think about what you would do to protect and launch your children into their destiny. That kind of love comes from God as we are made in His image. If we can love our children with an earthly love, can we even imagine the perfect love of our heavenly Father for us?

> *I have loved you with an everlasting love; I have drawn you with unfailing kindness* (Jeremiah 31:3).

Not only does God love you, but He also delights in you. He doesn't just love you because He has to. It's not as though our father says, "Well, my son died for you, so I guess I have to love you." He is the one who left the ninety-nine to pursue you. God is delighted in you, and He wants a relationship with you.

The Lord your God is with you, the Mighty Warrior who saves. He will take great delight in you; in his love he will no longer rebuke you, but will rejoice over you with singing (Zephaniah 3:17).

You are free. Your past is not only forgiven but washed away completely. Given a new nature, you have the ability to live a life of righteousness to the extent that you choose to do so.

It is for freedom that Christ has set us free. Stand firm, then, and do not let yourselves be burdened again by a yoke of slavery (Galatians 5:1).

Adopted into a new family, you have been given access to a new family line. Just like royal children, you can knock on the king's private chambers and know that the door will always be open for you. You are a coheir with Christ. In other words, you get the same inheritance that the Father gave to Jesus.

Now if we are children, then we are heirs—heirs of God and co-heirs with Christ (Romans 8:17).

Freedom comes with responsibilities. Our Father expects us to accept our true identity as responsible royal heirs and act as though we live in the castle, not the village. We are not to worry about things that worry common people. Our father wants us to accept our destiny and act in a way that reflects and glorifies Him. This does not imply laziness or entitlement. On the contrary, our time should be spent learning about the King and how His Kingdom rules so that we become like Him and act in a way that portrays His Kingdom accurately.

ACTION POINTS

1.   Do you see yourself as a favored, adopted royal heir? If not, why?

_____

_____

_____

_____

_____

2.   If behavior reflects identity, does your behavior indicate that you live in the village or the castle? If you said village, what part of your identity is rooted in an old mindset?

_____

_____

_____

_____

_____

3.   As you meditate on the following Scriptures, ask your heavenly papa to show you what He thinks about you. Write down what He says and then read this out loud repeatedly until it feels true to you.

   ▪ Ephesians 1-3

   ▪ John 1:12

   ▪ 1 Peter 2:9

   ▪ Romans 8:17

   ▪ Colossians 2:9-10

   ▪ Colossians 3:3

   ▪ 2 Timothy 1:7

_____

_____

_____

_____

_____

_____

_____

_____

4. Identity comes through spending time with your papa, and it's a process of revelation. The people I know who live with kingdom identity did not get this overnight but by a persistent pursuit of washing their mind with the truth of God's word. I would encourage you to keep a journal with a section dedicated to your identity in Christ that you can return to frequently.

Chapter 11

What Are You Wearing?

*"To be prepared for war is one of the most
effective means of preserving peace."*
—GEORGE WASHINGTON

Now that you know who you are, it's time to prepare yourself for battle like a professional soldier. My oldest son, Zachary, served in the US Army for eight years, including two tours in Iraq. His battle uniform while in Iraq included a helmet with eyewear for shrapnel and dust, a communication headset with earpiece, a bulletproof vest, and a Kevlar groin piece. In addition, he wore a load-bearing belt with straps to attach equipment, heavy duty treaded boots, desert camouflage uniform, and an M16 rifle with 210 rounds of ammunition. Other equipment he carried included a utility knife, flashlight, first aid kit, and a canteen or

Camelback for water. Zach wore protective gear (armor) to shield himself from battle threats. This was not optional or negotiable. Iraq could be extremely hot, and sand was devastating to equipment. It would have been so much more comfortable to wear shorts and sandals. However, Zach understood the threat and was prepared for battle conditions. He cleaned his M16 regularly, so he knew every part of his weapon. The weight and grip were comfortable and familiar because he practiced shooting regularly. Zach was prepared for battle conditions because he knew what type of weapons the enemy would use, where the attack would come from, and how the physical aspects of the terrain affected his risk. His gear and weapons were directly designed to protect him from his enemy.

We too live in a battle. However, many of us don't realize we are in a war with an enemy that seeks our destruction. We don't understand the battle conditions and the type of weapons our enemy will use. Some of us go into battle wearing inappropriate protection and weaponless, then wonder why we become injured and discouraged. Paul so eloquently writes:

> *Finally, be strong in the Lord and in his mighty power. Put on the full armor of God, so that you can take your stand against the devil's schemes. For our struggle is not against flesh and blood, but against the rulers, against the authorities, against the powers of this dark world and against the spiritual forces of evil in the heavenly realms. Therefore put on the full armor of God, so that when the day of evil comes, you may be able to stand your ground, and after you have done everything, to stand. Stand firm then, with the belt of truth buckled around your waist, with the breastplate of righteousness in place, and with your feet fitted with the readiness that comes from the gospel of peace. In addition to all this, take up the shield of faith, with which you can extinguish all the flaming arrows of the evil one. Take the helmet of salvation and the sword of the Spirit, which is the word of God. And pray in the Spirit on all occasions with all kinds of prayers and*

requests. With this in mind, be alert and always keep on praying for all the Lord's people (Ephesians 6:10-18).

Paul clearly describes the battle conditions we live in—forces in heavenly realms. God intends for us to win, but we have to stand and fight as prepared soldiers going into war. Going into combat wearing civvies and leaving our weapon behind is foolish and a recipe for disaster.

THE BELT OF TRUTH

When the belt we wear is riddled with lies instead of truth, it becomes difficult to keep our pants up. Instead of fighting, we are preoccupied with pulling up our sagging uniform so that tender areas are not exposed. Truth protects us and saves us time. When the enemy is shooting arrows at our exposed backside, we end up putting our weapon down as we scramble to pull our pants back into place. If we are girded with truth, our hands are free to go on the offensive with our sword. Zach's belt had straps that allowed him to carry additional equipment. His belt was load bearing. Truth, too, is load bearing. It can carry the weight of supplies we need into the battle.

Sharon, a frequent visitor to our office, is a persistent worrier. Although she professes to be a Christian, Sharon believes the lie that God is not always good. This stronghold in her mind causes her to view the world around her as threatening. Sharon is actually in good health for her age. She has a nice place to live and money to pay her bills, but she lives in a constant state of dread that something bad is going to happen to her. This underlying fear and anxiety exposes her backside to the accusations and lying darts of the enemy. Instead of using her sword, she is preoccupied with pulling out the darts and nursing her wounds. Sharon will not be able to stand firm in battle until she is wearing the belt of truth and believes that God is always good.

There are a variety of lies that can weaken our belt, as was described earlier. The lies that I most frequently encounter include—God is not always good; I am inadequate; I am not completely forgiven; I am a sinner, not a saint; I must always say yes; and God doesn't love me as described in Romans 8:38-39.

Lies are replaced by truth when we saturate ourselves in the word of God and immerse ourselves in His presence.

THE BREASTPLATE OF RIGHTEOUSNESS

Righteousness is like a bulletproof vest to our heart. It shields the organ that supplies life to every part of our body. This righteousness is twofold, and if not in correct order the breastplate (bulletproof vest) becomes ineffective.

These verses about our armor in Ephesians are probably quite familiar to you. I was taught that the breastplate of righteousness meant that I was to live a holy life, i.e., my righteousness protected me. It is true that we are to be holy as Christ is holy. However, self-righteousness is quite limited and not acceptable to God.

> *For all have sinned and fall short of the glory of God* (Romans 3:23).

The breastplate of righteousness Paul is referring to is the righteousness of Christ that is given to us as a gift through faith.

> *This righteousness is given through faith in Jesus Christ to all who believe* (Romans 3:22).

Jesus had some interesting things to say about righteousness. First, He said that those who were hungry for righteousness would be filled (see Matt. 5:6). Then in an extensive sermon about the uselessness of worry, He said that our priority should not be our concerns, but first *his kingdom and his righteousness* (see Matt. 6:33). Can you see it? When we don't seek *his kingdom and his righteousness,* our hearts become vulnerable to worldly desires, which then exposes us to sin and to worry. When we *wear the righteousness of Christ*, it acts like a bulletproof vest, protecting our heart from unholy desires because our focus becomes Christ and His Kingdom. The result is that we live a holy life because that is our desire, not our obligation. It is not a duty but love for our Savior who gave all so that we may be made righteous in Him.

> Righteousness is becoming in practice what you already are in position. —Dr. David Jeremiah

As we arise each morning, we remind ourselves that we are made righteous because of Christ. We put on our bulletproof vest by setting our heart and desires on *his kingdom and righteousness.* When the fiery arrows of accusation from the enemy come at us, they are deflected by a holy life anchored in the righteousness of Christ.

I suspect each of us can recall people we know who are reaping the results of a life lived without righteousness. Sin will take you out of the battle quickly. Gerald, an elder in a local church, came into the office a few months ago because he was having insomnia and anxiety. As I began to question him, he admitted that he was under a lot of stress. This patient was reluctant to tell me what was going on, but I finally got to the truth. He had been having an affair for over a year, and his wife had just found out and intended to leave him. He wasn't sure if he wanted to give up the affair, but he didn't want his wife to leave either. This guy was dying on the battlefield and didn't even realize it. Gerald's ability to stand against enemy forces has been completely dismantled. His sin had given the enemy permission to send oppressive spirits to taunt and torment him. This man didn't need medication, he needed repentance and counseling.

Gerald didn't just wake up one morning and decide to sin. He had developed a habit of not wearing his breastplate, the righteousness of Christ, over time. Because he did not seek first the Kingdom and righteousness of Christ, his heart was led astray by the desires of his flesh.

SHOES OF THE GOSPEL OF PEACE

Did you realize that the gospel (good news) of peace is the part of your armor that allows you to go into any part of the battle and be victorious? Can you imagine a soldier wearing flip-flops in a mine field? I see many people struggling in the battle, their mobility hampered due to inappropriate footwear.

Paul was describing the armor of a Roman soldier in Ephesians. These soldiers wore special boots studded with nails, which allowed them to hold their grip in difficult conditions. Their feet were not bruised or pierced by rocks, and they did not fall in slippery terrain. These soldiers were able to go wherever their commander sent orders.

How then shall they call on Him in whom they have not believed? And how shall they believe in Him of whom they have not heard? And how shall they hear without a preacher? And how shall they preach unless they are sent? As it is written: "How beautiful are the feet of those who preach the gospel of peace, who bring glad tidings of good things!" (Romans 10:14-15 NKJV)

Understanding the good news that reconciles us to God and brings peace to us is a life message that we take wherever we go. The good news of the gospel gives us purpose and drive, carrying us into every part of the world. No matter our calling or gifts, the gospel is our life message put on display for the world to see. Without our feet encased in this gospel of peace we go nowhere and accomplish little.

Did you notice that our message is not one of judgment or criticism? Have you met believers who wear shoes that proclaim another gospel—an angry, threatening gospel filled with rebuke? I've met these unhappy people in my practice. They often suffer from anger, anxiety, and depression, and they project this on others. The gospel they portray is both ineffective and undesirable.

Our life on this earth is a marathon, not a sprint. Paul describes it as such. Toward the end of his life, Paul talks about finishing the race (see 2 Tim. 4:7). In an earlier writing, he encourages us to run our race with intent to win (see 1 Cor. 9:24). To run such a long race over slippery, steep, and rocky terrain, littered with dangerous debris, we need to be shod with the good news of peace and reconciliation to our loving, heavenly Father.

THE SHIELD OF FAITH

Our faith in God, in what we cannot see, protects us from *all* of the fiery darts of the enemy. Faith has an offensive component to it. Did you notice that Paul said faith extinguished the darts of the enemy? We think of a shield deflecting darts, but our shield of faith has the supernatural ability to both deflect and extinguish darts.

The shield used by the Roman soldier was quite large, over three feet tall and wide, protecting both the soldier and the other parts of the armor he wore. With a simple shift in weight, the soldier could easily deflect arrows from all sides as well as knock the enemy backward with the metal knob that protruded from the center of the shield. The shield both protected the soldier and threw the enemy off balance.

When we face the arrows of doubt flung at us by the enemy, we can put up our shield of faith to extinguish the darts of the enemy. And if we are persistent in our faith we weaken the strategy of the enemy and send him in retreat. Jesus modeled this when He resisted Satan in the desert. After the third attempt, Satan retreated. It's important to remember that Satan has limited resources, and persistence wears him down. Faith will often cause him to retreat to an easier part of the battle.

So why do people go into battle without a shield? The root problem is unbelief. Unbelief kills faith. If you do not believe the promises of God, there is no access to a shield of faith. You go into battle completely exposed to the darts from every angle. You may be wearing other parts of your armor, but you lack the ability to not only protect yourself but to throw the enemy off of his plan. It becomes difficult to advance into enemy territory and gain ground without a shield. You are too busy trying to hide or duck from the darts. Your focus as a soldier becomes limited to survival instead of conquest.

Elizabeth comes into the office regularly with chronic anxiety and depression. Unfortunately, Elizabeth's condition has not responded to medications or counseling. I suspect that the lack of response to treatment is that her anxiety and depression have a spiritual root of unbelief. Elizabeth knows the promises of God. In fact, she can quote them. The problem is she does not *believe* that the promises hold true for her.

In Chapter 2, there is an analogy of the *trees* we allow to grow in our mind. There are two main trees that compete for growth and are not compatible with each other. These are the Trees of Faith and Unbelief. One will always dominate the other.

The dominant tree in Elizabeth's mind is unbelief, and this has become a stronghold or a place of dominion. Because of the unbelief, Elizabeth has no access to a shield of faith. Once she pulls up the Tree of Unbelief, which is rooted in lies, the Tree of Faith can grow. This is accomplished by meditating on God's word until you believe what is written.

Do you have an area in your life where you feel afraid? Chances are this is an area of unbelief that is controlled by a lie.

THE HELMET OF SALVATION

The helmet worn by the Roman soldier was designed to deflect the decapitating blows of the broadsword used by enemy forces. We too face an enemy that wants to cut off our head, and will do so if we don't wear our salvation helmet. So how does salvation protect our mind?

Salvation is encompassing. It has a past, present, and future component to it that protects us no matter where we are in the battle. We were saved (see Eph. 2:5). We are also in the process of being saved, and lastly we will be saved (see 1 Cor. 1:18; Matt. 10:22).

In an earlier chapter of Ephesians Paul writes:

> *But because of his great love for us, God, who is rich in mercy, made us alive with Christ even when we were dead in transgressions—it is by grace you have been saved. And God raised us up with Christ and seated us with him in the heavenly realms in Christ Jesus, in order that in the coming ages he might show the incomparable riches of his grace, expressed in his kindness to us in Christ Jesus. For it is by grace you have been saved, through faith—and this is not from yourselves, it is the gift of God—not by works, so that no one can boast* (Ephesians 2:4-9).

Our foundation as a believer in Jesus is that salvation is a gift from God given to us by grace, not by our efforts. This gift was freely given to us out of God's great love and mercy, not grudgingly because we forced his hand. The power of knowing and believing that *all* of our sins have been forgiven serves as a helmet when the enemy uses the broadsword of accusation against us.

Have you ever heard this lie?

"Remember when you failed because of (fill in the blank)? Your mistake disqualifies you. You will never be able to move past it."

If you are not wearing your salvation helmet, you are susceptible to that lie filling your mind, which leaves you decapitated, dead on the battlefield.

This lie is destroyed by washing our minds with the word, realizing that Jesus purchased our past, present, and future on the cross out of love, mercy, and grace and we are completely forgiven.

When Paul described putting on the helmet of salvation, he was talking to believers, people who had already been saved. Salvation is more than deliverance from past sin. It also keeps our minds protected in our present state. This is because salvation changes our identity. We are now joint heirs with Christ, seated in heavenly realms. This is a description of our current position, and not just a future state in the millennium.

Salvation also changes our nature. The old man died, and we were given a new nature. We now no longer live by the desires of our flesh. To the extent that we choose, we can live a life free from sin.

> *You, however, are not in the realm of the flesh but are in the realm of the Spirit, if indeed the Spirit of God lives in you* (Romans 8:9).

Last, our salvation helmet protects us for the future. We know that our current state is temporary, and we win in the end. This knowledge helps us endure difficulties and great persecution, even unto death. When the enemy comes at us with lies that tell us we will be defeated and that he is greater than our God, our helmet protects our mind from the lies. We know that the truth of our salvation is greater than the facts of our circumstances.

The enormity of what Jesus did for us on the cross—purchasing our past, present, and future salvation—is not well understood by most believers in Christ. This lack of understanding causes many believers to go without their helmet into the battle. These victims are open to the accusations and discouragement of the enemy. Is it any wonder that there are so many headless believers strewn on the battlefield, overcome by anxiety and depression, unable to do the work of the Father?

THE SWORD OF THE SPIRIT

The sword is my favorite part of the armor because of both its offensive and defensive capability. Obviously, all of the armor is necessary. We wouldn't just go into battle naked with a sword! But the sword is what allows us to defeat enemy forces and take territory, not just defend ground we've already won.

As Paul wrote to the Ephesians while in prison in Rome, he had plenty of opportunities to study the armor of the most feared warrior of his time. The sword that the Roman soldier used was deadly and meant for close combat. This sword was both defensive and offensive. It was sharp on each edge and had a tapered point that could pierce armor. The word of God, our sword of the Spirit, is just like the sword the Roman soldier used.

> *For the word of God is alive and active. Sharper than any double-edged sword, it penetrates even to dividing soul and spirit, joints and marrow; it judges the thoughts and attitudes of the heart* (Hebrews 4:12).

God's word is alive today, and it carries within it the supernatural ability to fulfill the promise it declares. When you wield the truth of the word, "No weapon formed against you will prosper" (Isa. 54:17). Your words are slicing deep into enemy forces that are attempting to use fear to get you to crumble in defeat.

Unfortunately, you can't use the word of God if you aren't familiar with it. A soldier doesn't go into battle without picking up his weapon, examining every aspect of the weapon, caring for it, and above all practicing with it. In other words, the soldier *knows* the trustworthiness and capability of his weapon. He knows how, when, and where to use it so well that he can grab it from a dead sleep and wield it in the dark. He knows the grip, the angle, and the position to thrust to defeat his enemy. Oh, if we could know the word of God like this. What if the word of God was so familiar to you that you could use it half asleep, in the dark, hungry, tired, and pressed on all sides? What if no matter your circumstance, you were so familiar with the Word that you knew the promise for everything you faced? There would be no enemy that could stand against you.

There is great power in the *spoken* word. The next chapter outlines this principle more clearly. Don't just silently read the word, but speak it out loud. Find the Scriptures that speak to your situation and speak them out loud until they ring true in your heart and you feel the enemy quiver. This is how you practice using your sword. You apply the word so that it washes your mind and becomes part of you. It rolls off your lips easily; it is familiar and it's nearby, easy for you to grab when the enemy springs out at you in a surprise attack.

PRAY IN THE SPIRIT

Paul told us to pray in all occasions. Do you live a lifestyle of prayer that's spirit-led?

Zach's uniform included a headset with an earpiece—a communication device. This earpiece allowed him to be in contact with the leader of his unit and to *hear* changes in orders or battle conditions. Battle conditions are often unstable. Soldiers who become isolated from their commander don't have access to the latest information, and may not know about a newly discovered IED (improvised explosive device) up ahead. They may be operating on outdated information.

This analogy applies in the spirit realm as well. Our heavenly Father sees the whole battlefield while we only see our current condition. Strategies and plans can change. The only way to know is to pray and find out what God is saying daily.

In summary, what are you wearing? Do you have the belt of truth around your waist? Are you wearing the breastplate of righteousness and the shoes of the gospel of peace? Is your head protected with the helmet of salvation and are you using your shield of faith? Are you familiar and practiced with the sword of the word of God, and are you in communication with the Father? If you are missing any piece of your armor, you are susceptible to all sorts of enemy schemes that can result in anxiety and depression.

ACTION POINTS

1. As you think about the belt of truth holding everything together, are there any lies you believe that weaken your belt? Write them out and find the corresponding Scripture that counters the lie.

   _____

   _____

   _____

   _____

2. Are you wearing the breastplate of the righteousness of Christ? If not, then why? What do you need to do to put it on?

   _____

   _____

   _____

   _____

3. Are you seeking first His Kingdom and His righteousness? Do you see righteousness as a duty or as a position you expect to live from out of love?

   _____

   _____

   _____

   _____

4. Are you wearing the shoes of the gospel of peace? Is your life message prepared to take you into all of the world, reconciling people to God? If not, then what shoes are you wearing and what do you need to do to change them?

   _____

   _____

   _____

   _____

5. How big is your shield of faith? Are there any strongholds of unbelief in your mind that make faith difficult to access? If so, then what is the truth you need to apply?

    _____

    _____

    _____

    _____

6. Are you fully wearing the helmet of salvation—the past, present, and future? If not, what are the areas that you need to apply the fullness of what Jesus did for you on the cross?

    _____

    _____

    _____

    _____

7. How sharp is your sword of the Spirit? Do you spend time meditating and speaking the word to your circumstances? If not, then what Scriptures is God emphasizing? Write them out and get so familiar with them, they roll off your tongue with little effort.

    _____

    _____

    _____

    _____

8. Are you wearing your communication headset and earpiece? Are you living a lifestyle of spirit-led prayer? If not, what can you do to change this? Spend time with the Father to hear what He has to say about this.

    _____

    _____

    _____

    _____

Chapter 12

Express the Word

"Death and life are in the power of the tongue
and those who love it will eat its fruits."
—Solomon, Proverbs 18:21 NKJV

Now that we are wearing the appropriate armor for battle, let's discuss another battle tool that we have at our disposal. This tool requires mastery as it can be used to bring death or life. Some people use this weapon incorrectly and unknowingly bring destruction on themselves and others.

One of the most critically important tools available to us is our speech. If we can master our tongue, we can direct the course of our life and the lives of others. Although ships are large and driven by powerful winds and waves, they are steered by a small rudder (see James 3:4). We are like these ships. There may be powerful forces pulling or pushing at us, but we steer our lives with the rudder of our words.

In the same way, we choose life or death each time we open our mouths to speak. Our words are that powerful. Think about it. God *spoke* the universe into existence. There was the actual power of creation released in the spoken word. Jesus Himself was the Word become flesh (see John 1:14).

Words create worlds, as my friend Kris Vallotton says. What we say has the power to change the atmosphere and shift our direction—good or bad. Our speech can create faith in us or promote unbelief. Words can invite the presence and the power of God into our situation or invite oppression and fear from demonic beings. For this reason, we need to actively promote speech that lines up with God's truth and His promises and guard our tongue against speaking curses. Just like the captain of a ship in a storm does not allow the wind and waves to push him at will but instead steers the rudder to a safe course, we too must direct the rudder of our tongue to a safe course.

> *And the tongue is a fire, a world of unrighteousness. The tongue is set among our members, staining the whole body, setting on fire the entire course of life, and set on fire by hell* (James 3:6 ESV).

I groaned under my breath as I reviewed my patient schedule. Margie, a 68-year-old healthy patient, was coming in that morning. I knew that when I stepped into the room, I'd hear a magnified version of how awful her symptoms were, a statement of how these things always happened to her, and a prediction that her symptoms could be a sign of cancer or some other fatal condition. When I gave her a minor diagnosis and a simple treatment plan, she was not convinced. I sighed. There's no pleasing this patient. She sucks the life, hope, and joy right out of the room. I can't wait to get away from her, and I'm sure others feel that way as well. The entire atmosphere around this patient is created by her words.

*Whoever guards his mouth preserves his life; he who opens wide
his lips comes to ruin* (Proverbs 13:3 ESV).

Fortunately, Peter was on my schedule that day as well. Peter is not well. He has an incurable blood cancer, and his life expectancy is only a year or so. But Peter has such a positive attitude, and his speech is full of hope and recognition of the wonderful things in his life. He always asks me about my family and tells me something funny. When Peter walks into the room, the entire atmosphere becomes full of life, hope, laughter, and joy. He sets a course with his tongue that pushes himself and others away from despair and depression—unlike Margie, who allows the rudder of her tongue to go with the storm. What atmosphere do you create with your tongue?

*Gracious words are a honeycomb, sweet to the soul and healing
to the bones* (Proverbs 16:24).

William, a 72-year-old gentleman who is conscientious about his health, came into the office recently. He has elevated blood pressure, and this worries him. Quite a few things worry William. I know that when he's on my schedule I'm going to get behind for the rest of the morning. Not only am I going to hear about his physical problems, but I'm also going to hear a list of complaints about the government, Obamacare, and a variety of other issues he has no control over. It's no wonder this patient has elevated blood pressure. He's quite angry, and his words create an atmosphere of hostility and offense. I take a deep breath and ask the Holy Spirit for grace and peace as I walk into the room. On this particular day, I gently interrupted the tirade and asked William why he was so angry. Why did he have the right to be angry? I reminded him that Christ had forgiven him of his transgressions. As he looked at me, his countenance changed. The truth of what Christ had done for Him penetrated his mind. His speech began to change, and the atmosphere of the room shifted.

For by your words you will be justified, and by your words you will be condemned (Matthew 12:37 ESV).

In what atmosphere would you like to live? I expect that we all want to live in a place of joy, hope, and peace. We create this from our speech. Even as God created the world with His words, we create the world around us with our words. Our words also affect others. People want to be around those who offer encouraging, kind, gracious, and humorous words. We like being around those who make us feel good and make us laugh.

From the fruit of a man's mouth his stomach is satisfied; he is satisfied by the yield of his lips (Proverbs 18:20 ESV).

Just because we have a thought, doesn't mean we should speak that thought into the atmosphere. I'm speaking to those of you who externally process! So many of us allow our tongues to speak any thought that runs across the surface of our brain. We neglect to test the accuracy of the thought and the effect of our words on others. Our words, though unintentional, result in consequences. Author Jodi Picoult states:

Words [are] like eggs dropped from great heights: You can no more call them back then ignore the mess they leave when they fall.[1]

There are many warnings and exhortations throughout the Scripture about what we allow our mouths to speak. There is no other part of the body that is discussed as much as the tongue.

Words cannot be recalled. Once spoken they land and produce something, similar to the principle of planting seeds. I have a raised vegetable garden that I cultivate regularly. I'm very selective of the type of seeds I put in my garden. I choose which seeds, how many, and their location in the ground. I don't haphazardly toss any old seeds into the bed and expect to grow tomatoes, cucumbers, and peppers. It's very easy to grow weeds—no effort at all. And that's exactly what most people have, not only in their yards but in their minds. The reason is that they unknowingly sow word seeds of destruction that outcompete the good seeds of joy, hope, and peace.

In my garden, I pull up the weeds as soon as I see them. I don't want them to go to seed and produce more weeds. If I put it off a week or two, I have a lot more work to do. This is what we need to do with our words. We need to pull up the negative words continually and selectively speak words of faith and hope.

> *Set a guard, O Lord, over my mouth; keep watch over the door of my lips!* (Psalm 141:3 ESV)

Bill Johnson says if we control what we think, we don't have to control what we say. I think most of us are more at the level of just trying to keep a lid on our tongue, but Bill has it right.

> *For out of the abundance of the heart the mouth speaks* (Matthew 12:34 NKJV).

Our words are a reflection of our thoughts. This goes back to the principle of *taking every thought captive to the obedience of Christ*. If you find yourself speaking weedy words, chances are your thoughts are not obedient to Christ.

What fruit do you want to eat? In general, we are currently eating the fruit of previous thoughts and words. If you are not enjoying what you're eating, you need to change the tree you are allowing to grow in the garden of your mind. You can't get peaches from a lemon tree!

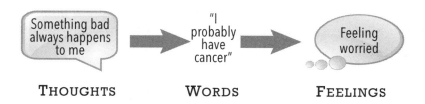

Up to this point, I've primarily discussed how our words can negatively affect us. It's true that we can prevent a lot of damage by simply keeping our mouths shut. However, words are a powerful tool for creating hope, peace, faith, and life. Remember, both life and death are in the power of the tongue. Words that declare God's truth and God's promises can bring us hope and life.

> *So faith comes from hearing, and hearing through the word of Christ* (Romans 10:17 ESV).

It is important that we hear with our ears words that declare God's promises. Most of us probably read God's word silently. The words we read provide information to our brain through a specific pathway. However, reading and speaking the words aloud activates additional pathways that create neural connectivity. Pathways that are interconnected are stronger and have better retention in our memory. There is something powerful about reading the Scriptures aloud. The truth becomes more real in our brain. Declaring God's word aloud also reminds demonic beings of what God has said.

I can remember going through a very difficult time many years ago when my very core and character were tested. Nurse practitioners had just received the ability to write prescriptions in California. Up until that time, we had to call medications in to the pharmacy or write them on a pad and find a physician to sign them. I was one of the first NPs to prescribe in the Redding area, and it was exciting. The clinic where I worked often found the MDs and NPs treating family members of staff for minor things, and I wrote a prescription for a fluoride supplement and albuterol inhaler refill for my son. The pharmacist reported this to my employer, and they called me on the carpet. They weren't aware of the new changes in the law and had no idea I could prescribe at all. And even though the medications were what I would typically use in family practice, they felt it was unethical for me to prescribe medications for a family member who wasn't a patient at the clinic. They were right. I was devastated, and I resigned. But even worse, they reported me to the BRN (Board of Registered Nursing), and I had to endure two years of waiting as the BRN investigated. I was such a by-the-book person, and I never got in trouble. Embarrassment overwhelmed me. I found another job and was up front with my new boss about the BRN investigation. Fortunately, my new employer thought the whole thing was overblown and was quite supportive. In the end, the BRN made me take some hours of continuing education on prescribing and placed me on probation for two years. But there is a permanent mark on my record and to this day every time I renew my DEA licensure or register with a new insurance company I have to explain this BRN disciplinary process on my application.

The point in telling this story is to tell you what I did when I lost my job and had to endure two long years of waiting for the BRN decision. The "what if?" scenarios would race through my head. What if my patients found out? What would happen if the BRN made me pay a large fine that I couldn't afford? Even worse, what if they pulled my license—all those years of school for nothing? What would people think of me? Would they ever trust me again? It was a nightmare that wouldn't quit. I found myself on my knees in prayer and tears. How could I have been so stupid? Why didn't I see it at the time? How would I ever recover my reputation? I buried myself in the Scriptures, and I would camp on a Scripture that would highlight itself to me. The Holy Spirit was so comforting and totally met me in this crisis. He would show me promises in the Word. My biggest challenge was choosing to believe that what He said was true, and my biggest foe was unbelief. Was he really good on His promises?

I finally decided to throw all of my eggs in one basket. I couldn't live in double-mindedness because that will make you crazy. I didn't have much to lose, so I chose to believe that what he said was completely, unequivocally true. I knew I had to get those promises inside me. So I would take a Scripture, and I would read it out loud, sometimes 20 times or more. My mouth declared the truth over and over again until my brain (soul) would agree with my heart (spirit). I would not stop until the truth resonated in my mind, and I could *feel* the hope, joy, and peace that the truth would bring. Remember, feelings are often a bit delayed, but feelings are very important. We don't believe something to be true unless it *feels* true. Often it's a matter of time. Instead of reading through a bunch of promises, take one Scripture that you know in your head to be true and camp on it. Meditate on it and speak it out loud. Let the feelings of that truth that your spirit understands penetrate your mind and change how you think. Repeat this process over and over again and it will change you. The truth of Scripture becomes your new reality, not your circumstances.

Oh, the peace that would flood my soul. The truth I knew in my soul and spirit was superior to the facts of my circumstances. My spoken words brought life and renewed my thinking.

The level of intimacy and trust I developed during that time changed me permanently. I wouldn't trade it for anything as it's made me who I am today. I might walk with a limp, but I know who my Redeemer is. One morning I read:

> *You will tread on the lion and the cobra; you will trample the great lion and the serpent* (Psalm 91:13).

I was encouraged by the Psalm and didn't think too much about it. But a couple of hours later, I was out sweeping the back patio and found two young rattlesnakes close to my back door. I can remember screaming and dancing a small jig, but there was no one to hear me. We lived out in the country, and my husband was at work. I had two little boys who were in the house at the time, so I had to do something. I ran to the garage grabbed a shovel and still screaming and jumping crushed the two snakes. After the adrenaline had cleared and I could think, the Holy Spirit reminded me of the Scripture above that mentioned trampling snakes twice. I laughed. I knew in the deepest part of me that what I was facing would be trampled, and however it turned out I would be safe. Even as I write this, the same peace, confidence, and trust pour through my mind as it did that day. *He is faithful.* I know in the deepest part of me that that is true no matter what I face.

> *"The word is near you, in your mouth and in your heart"* (that is, the word of faith that we proclaim) (Romans 10:8 ESV).

The word needs to not just be in our heart or mind but in our mouth. When we speak aloud, we are telling our brain what to think. One of the most powerful things we can do is camp on one of God's promises and repeatedly declare it with our mouths. Initially, those words may seem empty, but I promise you, as you read them aloud over and over, the truth of God's word will penetrate your brain and renew your mind. The purpose of this exercise is to read the words until they *feel* true. Remember, there is often a delay between thought and a feeling. So keep declaring until your feelings line up with your thoughts. This method is a practical way to take your thoughts captive to the obedience of Christ.

> *If you abide in my word, you are truly my disciples, and you will know the truth, and the truth will set you free* (John 8:31-32 ESV).

We need to abide in the word. That means we need to live in the word. God's word is alive and has the power to transform our minds.

> *The words that I have spoken to you are spirit and life* (John 6:63 ESV).

I wonder how many of us truly abide in the word. How often do we allow the word to penetrate and wash our minds? I know I am guilty of just skimming over the surface of God's word or just looking to the Bible for information. But God's word is different from other words. God's word is alive, and it is more than information. God's word is revelation and transformation if we take the time to meditate on it thoroughly.

> *Let the words of my mouth and the meditation of my heart be acceptable in your sight, O Lord, my rock and my redeemer* (Psalm 19:14 ESV).

ACTION POINTS

1. What are the curses you've spoken over your circumstances? Repent over each one and ask the Lord for the truth.

_____

_____

2. What are the Scriptures that speak to you or that God has highlighted to you as promises for your life? Write them out. Place them on your mirror and your fridge. Speak them out loud frequently. Do it over and over again until your soul and your spirit agree.

_____

_____

_____

_____

_____

NOTE

1. Jodi Picoult, *Salem Falls* (New York: Washington Square Press, 2001), 112.

Chapter 13

Remember

"You can go as far as your mind lets you. What you believe, remember, you can achieve."
—MARY KAY ASH

Although I've placed this chapter in spiritual tools for renewal of the mind, remembering has a strong psychological component as well. One of the most powerful tools we have to renew our mind is to remember and remind ourselves of what God has already done for us in the past. We've learned our identity and how to wear our armor and use our weapons, but sometimes we can be so overwhelmed with fear it's all we can do to stay upright in the battle. The simple skill of telling our brain to remember (meditate on) past victories causes faith to arise and give us the courage to go on.

I will remember the deeds of the Lord; yes, I will remember your miracles of long ago. I will consider all your works and meditate on all your mighty deeds (Psalm 77:11-12).

To meditate means to ponder or to mull something over in your mind. Another definition of meditation is to ruminate. Meditation is a powerful tool that has been used by the church for millennia and it should be part of our daily walk with God. Here are just a few of the numerous Scriptures on this subject:

*We **meditate** on your unfailing love* (Psalm 48:9 NLT).

*I will **meditate** on all Your work* (Psalm 77:12 NASB).

*So I will **meditate** on Your wonders* (Psalm 119:27 NASB).

Everyone meditates. In fact, we do it all day long. It's just a matter of subject material. There are several research studies that show reminiscing is good for our minds. Researchers at the University of Southampton found that people who indulged in nostalgic thinking had the highest scores of happiness, self-esteem, and social bonding.[1] Thinking about past positive events can reduce anxiety. It allows us to travel back in time and regenerate the feelings of victory, love, faith, or accomplishment we felt at a previous point in the past. Drawing on prior experiences reminds us of our strengths and our ability to cope with difficult situations. A study by Fred Bryant, professor of psychology at Loyola University, showed that people who reminisced for ten minutes, twice daily, had greater scores of happiness than the control group.[2]

As said in a previous chapter, thoughts generate chemicals that produce feelings. Your brain does not need to distinguish the past from the present to generate feelings of happiness. As you *relive* the moment, those chemicals that were released in your brain during the original event are released again. You can enjoy the moment as though the event were happening to you right now. It's a great tool—easy to use and always accessible.

Every one of us has had experiences throughout our lives where God has rescued, delivered, encouraged, comforted, healed, and loved us. How soon we forget. We become like the men of Ephraim.

> *Though armed with bows, turned back on the day of battle; they did not keep God's covenant and refused to live by his law. They **forgot** what He had done, the wonders he had shown them* (Psalm 78:9-11).

The Scriptures are replete with stories of people who forgot the tremendous miracles of their past and fell into fear. Remember the Israelites in the wilderness? These are the same people who were miraculously delivered out of the clutches of Pharaoh, walked through a parted sea, were fed with manna daily, given water from a rock, etc. How quickly they fell into murmuring and unbelief. It's astounding, really, except that we do the same thing.

Many years ago, when my children were just babies, my husband and I moved to Redding from southern California for a job relocation. Just as we moved, the housing bubble burst and we found ourselves unable to sell our home. We were making a large mortgage payment on our home in southern California and paying rent for a home in Redding on one income. We were confident the house would sell, and we had several months of savings on which to live. However, as three turned into six months, our savings dwindled. Even though we substantially dropped the price on the house, there were still no offers. I prayed liked I'd never prayed before. My husband and I knew we had done the right thing by moving to Redding, but we would soon be facing foreclosure. I had never failed to pay a bill on time, and the thought of losing the house was unimaginable to me. I could remember coming to a point in prayer where I told God it was okay if he took the house. I would love Him and serve Him all my days, no matter what happened. I came into this world naked, and I would leave the same way. A tremendous burden lifted from my spirit, and I was filled with peace. Over the next two months, unusual checks began to show up in the mail. We received money from an insurance over payment from the previous year, which helped us make the mortgage payment one month. But even still there came a moment when I looked at the budget and realized that if I paid the tithe, there would be no money for groceries that week. I sat there at the kitchen table debating for a few minutes. Do I trust God? Here was the test. If I pay my tithe, which I've always done, I will not be able to buy groceries this week. I remember saying, "God, you've said you are faithful, and you do not leave your children begging for bread. I choose to believe you are true to your word." So I wrote the check for tithe. A couple of days later we received a check for a property tax refund from Los Angeles County. I was astonished, as it was completely unexpected. This kind of thing happened several more times, and my faith in God was solidified to the degree that it changed how I thought about Him. The next month our home sold and the eight-month struggle was over.

I will never forget that experience. It is burned in my brain. Even as I write this, I can remember that feeling of stepping off the ledge when I wrote that tithe check. I remember the fear and the final giving over. I felt like I had been dragged—kicking and screaming, heels dug in, unwilling to go down the path. I remember that moment of giving over and putting not just some, but all of my trust in Him, the one who is faithful. I remember the joy and surprise of finding those crazy checks in the mail, and I remember the feelings of faith overwhelming my spirit and mind. That experience is mine to keep and to savor, to pull out when I need it again.

JOURNAL YOUR TESTIMONIES

When you are in crisis, it can become difficult to remember past victories. Emotional stress can make it hard to both focus and remember. Mark came into the office requesting to be checked for a hormonal imbalance as he was having memory problems. He had gotten a promotion at work, and the new job duties felt overwhelming to him. I asked him if he felt anxious or depressed and he said no. However, as I asked about racing thoughts, feelings of tenseness, and insomnia, he agreed that he had all of those things. Mark had anxiety, and when the brain is anxious it doesn't remember very well. The information comes in, but the brain is like a large sieve, and most of the information just doesn't stick when you're anxious. All of Mark's lab tests were normal. We talked about proper diet, sleep, exercise, and some short-term counseling to get him back on track. Mark did not need medication as his anxiety was situational. With a bit of time his anxiety lessened, and his memory returned to normal.

This difficulty of remembering when you're in a crisis is why it's important to record your testimonies. If you haven't done so, start a journal of all of the testimonies in your life. You can also record the testimonies of others. God is no respecter of persons. What He has done for others He will do for you. This way, when you get into a crisis you can pull out your journal and remind yourself of God's faithfulness. Begin to meditate and relive those victories like David did. You may need to read that journal over and over again. Keep doing it until faith arises.

Anna had been a patient of mine for years. She struggled with recurrent anxiety because of the poor choices made by her adult children. Her children were not serving God, and their addictions and failed marriages had caused tremendous upheaval for both themselves and her grandchildren. Unfortunately, this is an all too frequent story in our society today. Many grandparents are taking care of their grandchildren due to the substance abuse of the parents. Anna felt hopeless in that there was nothing she could do in the natural to change the situation for her children or her grandchildren. I asked Anna to tell me what God had done for her in the past. It took a while for her to remember, as she was so overwhelmed with the current situation. Slowly, she began to tell me of how God had miraculously saved her in a car accident many years prior. That story then generated another, then another. Her countenance began to change, and hope began to arise. I asked her to tell me the promises that God had given to her for her children. I believe God gives each of us promises for our children and we have permission to pray and speak that identity over our children. I encouraged Anna to focus on what God had done and the promises He had made instead of focusing on what God had not done yet. This is an important key: *Focus on what God has done, not on your problem.*

David used this technique to encourage himself. As you read the Psalms, you will notice that at the beginning of the psalm David is often discouraged. He is quite honest about his feelings, describing himself as weak and dying. Yet, he reminds his soul (his mind) about past victories in the Lord. This begins to stir up hope, which then turns into declarations of God's faithfulness and ultimate victory. By the end of the psalm, he is full of faith and encouragement. There is no reason we cannot use this technique as well. It starts with the simple act of remembering and meditating on the truth. What God has done, He can do again. He does not change. He is faithful and fulfills His word.

> *He has caused his wonders to be remembered; the Lord is gracious and compassionate...he* **remembers** *his covenant forever* (Psalm 111:4-5).

Have you ever felt like God didn't hear you? Or that your soul could not be comforted? Have you ever felt so troubled that you could not speak? You are not alone. David describes feeling like this in Psalm 77. He moved himself out of this state by remembering God's past favor, love, mercy, compassion, promises, and deeds. David's spirit told his soul (mind) to change what he was thinking about. It wasn't easy.

> *I remembered you, O God, and I groaned* (Psalm 77:3).

But he forced himself to continue with this train of thought:

My heart meditated and my spirit asked: "Will the Lord reject forever?" (Psalm 77:7)

About halfway through the psalm, David's entire tone changes. He declares God's ways with strength, and he becomes full of hope and faith. His feelings and his words changed as his thoughts changed. This is a beautiful example of self-discipline. David did not allow his feelings to run his thought life. He forced himself to remember, even though it was difficult.

What a powerful tool and so simple. We can all do this. When you are going through a difficult time and all you can see is the problem in front of you, step back and remember what God has done for you in the past. Don't allow your feelings to overwhelm your thought life. As you do this, your problem will be overshadowed by God's power, love, and faithfulness toward you. You will begin to get the correct perspective.

Perspective is critical because there is a difference between *truth* and facts. We humans get caught up in facts and forget *the truth*. It's not that facts aren't true, but there is the truth and then there is the *greater truth*. Not all truth is equal, and we often forget that. We know that sin requires judgment. This fact is true. However, mercy triumphs over judgment. Both judgment and mercy are true, but mercy is a higher truth. Faith, hope, and love remain, yet the greatest of these is love. Love is obviously a higher truth. We know that we will have trials and persecution in this life because we have an enemy, but the greater truth is that God in us is greater than anything Satan can throw at us.

There are the facts of our situation—financial hardship, health crisis, loss of a job, family discord, etc. The *greater truth* is that God is Lord of all. The *greater truth* is that there is no problem our loving Father cannot fix. There is no disease He cannot heal. There is no child who is so far away from God that He cannot be reached. What is the *greater truth* of the situation you are facing? Beloved, fix your eyes on this *truth*, not on the facts.

HOW BIG IS YOUR GOD?

Bill Johnson says you can tell the size of a person by the size of the problem it takes to discourage him. I know people who are constantly discouraged by the smallest of things and I know people who are facing great challenges with hope and joy. Obviously, there is a conscious choice of what we decide to think about. It's not that we ignore our problems. It's just that we put our focus on God, who is greater and more powerful than anything we are facing.

It all comes down to perspective. How big is your God? So many people have a small or a distant God and a great big close-up devil. Does it feel like Satan and God are duking it out and it's a fairly even match? Or perhaps you feel God is just plain absent? Remember, feelings and truth don't necessarily agree! When our feelings are running the show, we have to say *stop*. It is now time to forcefully set our thoughts and attention on what God has said or what God is saying about our current situation.

God and Satan are not equal opponents. Satan is a created being, on par with Michael and Gabriel, the archangels. He has some power, but he is not God's counterpart by any means. He's also outnumbered in the heavenly realm two to one. We have been told:

> *You, dear children, are from God and have overcome them, because the one who is in you is greater than the one who is in the world* (1 John 4:4).

God can crush Satan without lifting a finger. Another *greater truth* is that we never face battles alone.

Be strong and courageous. Do not be afraid or terrified because of them, for the Lord your God goes with you; he will never leave you nor forsake you (Deuteronomy 31:6).

God has said, "Never will I leave you; never will I forsake you" (Hebrews 13:5).

To be completely honest, it all comes down to faith or unbelief. I believe that this issue is the main battlefield of the mind, and each of us deals with it at some level. Do we choose to believe what God has said? Or do we choose to put our trust in our circumstances or the "facts" of our situation? Much anxiety and depression is a direct result of our unbelief in the goodness and faithfulness of God toward us or in what other people may think about us. The fear and dread of our circumstances overwhelm us with unbelief. God never punishes His children. He may discipline us, but even then it is done with mercy and love for our benefit.

Dear one, you are not alone. Give over and put your trust in God. He is bigger and better than you know. He loves you with an everlasting love, and He has your best in mind. He can work out any, and I mean any situation to your good. No trial you are facing is too big for Him. He has a solution, and He will give you grace for the situation you are facing.

Our main problem again is perspective. We are unable to see the entire story as we have a very limited view of our circumstances. God sees the big picture and knows the end from the beginning. We only see what's right in front of us. But what we can do is turn our attention from the problem to the solution—our beloved Father, our Redeemer, the lover of our souls. The more we look at Him, the bigger He gets. The bigger He gets, the smaller our problem becomes. We need to get up high and get heaven's perspective on our problem. Things look much different the higher you are. As we turn our attention to Him, our faith, our courage, and our strength increase.

> *Never let the problem you are facing*
> *become bigger than God's presence.*
> —BILL JOHNSON

Feelings are not evil. In fact, feelings are quite useful as a thermometer for your thought life. Are you feeling worried, hopeless, and overwhelmed? It's time to get back into His presence. And an easy way to do that is to remember your past victories and those of others.

> *I can't afford to have a thought about*
> *myself that He isn't thinking.*
> —BILL JOHNSON

What does God think about you? What does God say and think about your situation? You can find out if you meditate, remember, and get into His presence.

In summary, to remember what God has done is a powerful tool we can use to correct our perspective. When we remember we are meditating, setting our thoughts on God's love for us, His ways, and His works. This changes our focus from the facts of our circumstances to the greater truth of the one who is in control.

ACTION POINTS

1. How much time do you spend daily meditating on God's love, on all that He has done, and on His wonders? If this is a weak area for you, think about where you can carve out just 10 minutes to incorporate this into your routine. It may be as simple as meditating during your commute time or while you're doing chores.

2. Journal your testimonies. Spend some time and begin to remember what God has done for you. Write the stories out. Can you remember

how you felt? What did God teach you during that season? Savor these memories. Go back to them frequently. As in the ancient days when the Israelites made stone memorials after a victory so they would not forget, you also have monuments in your life that need to be frequently visited.

3. What is the greater truth of your situation?

_____

_____

_____

_____

4. How big is your God? What is the truth? What does God say about your situation?

_____

_____

_____

_____

NOTES

1. Tim Wildschut et al., "Nostalgia: Content, Triggers, Functions," *Journal of Personality and Social Psychology* 91, no. 5 (2006): 975-93, doi:10.1037/0022-3514.91.5.975.

2. Fred B. Bryant, Colette M. Smart, and Scott P. King, "Using the Past to Enhance the Present: Boosting Happiness Through Positive Reminiscence," *Journal of Happiness Studies* 6, no. 3 (2005): 227-60, doi:10.1007/s10902-005-3889-4.

Chapter 14

Gratitude and Generosity

*"Gratitude makes sense of our past, brings peace
for today and creates a vision for tomorrow."*
—MELODY BEATTIE

Gratitude is the natural extension of remembering. As we think about what God has done and is currently doing in our lives, gratitude fills our heart and renews our mind. Thankfulness is not just a sentimental feeling but a virtue. Regardless of circumstances, gratitude becomes an aggressive stance taken to express faith in the goodness of God.

Thankfulness focuses your thoughts and your attention to what is right and good in the world around you. As you think about the wonderful blessings in your life, chemicals are released in the brain that give you a sense of well-being. As mentioned earlier, every feeling you experience (positive or negative) is the direct result of chemicals being released due to the activation of a particular pathway in the brain. If you want joy and peace to be constant companions, think about and express your thanksgiving and gratitude to God and the people around you on a frequent basis. Make it a regular habit and those pathways will become a positive stronghold in your mind.

When we lack a thankful heart, we open ourselves up to sin. In *Spiritual Java,* Bill Johnson points out that thankfulness allows us to know God, and that without thankfulness the heart becomes futile and without purpose.[1] Jonathan Edwards, the leader of the great revival in Wales, claimed that gratitude was one of the most accurate ways to find God's presence in your life.

Anyone can complain and point to the negative things in the world around them. It takes no faith or discernment to be negative, and unfortunately it's a common and accepted practice in our culture. Although initially it may feel awkward to express gratitude for the simple things in your life, with a bit of time and effort you can always find something to be thankful for, no matter your circumstances.

Our culture trains us to look for what is wrong in the world around us so that we can make corrections and fix problems. Media surrounds us with stories of crime, crises, scandals, and other negative issues because that's what sells. It makes you wonder what our world would look like if our media focused on stories of excellence, goodness, and heroism. Being thankful and looking for what is good in the world around us goes against our cultural norm. There is a conscious effort we must make that is similar to rowing a boat upstream. It would be so much easier just to drift and go with the negative flow, and this is what most people do. Gratitude may not be our cultural norm, but it is our spiritual norm, and the more we do it, the easier and more natural it becomes.

A research study done by Emmons and McCullough demonstrated that people who kept a daily gratitude journal showed higher levels of alertness, enthusiasm, determination, optimism, and energy when compared to groups who either recorded events of the day or who recorded unpleasant things that happened during their day.[2] The grateful group also experienced less depression and stress, exercised more, had healthier coping strategies and problem solving, slept better, and were more likely to help others. Obviously gratitude is good for the mind, body, and spirit.

Gratitude and praise are inextricably linked. As you meditate on what God has done for you, feelings of thankfulness will overwhelm your heart, and praise to God follows as a natural outpouring of your spirit. Read the Psalms and notice how often David moved himself from a state of despair to a state of faith and joy by both remembering what God had done and by offering thanksgiving and praise. In Psalm 7, David begins with this statement:

Lord my God, I take refuge in you; save and deliver me from all who pursue me, or they will tear me apart like a lion and rip me to pieces with no one to rescue me (Psalm 7:1-2).

Then about halfway through this psalm, David begins to remember and declare God's character. By the end of the psalm he declares:

I will give thanks to the Lord because of his righteousness; I will sing the praises of the name of the Lord Most High (Psalm 7:17).

David was able to move himself from a place of feeling overwhelmed by his current circumstances to a place of gratitude. From thankfulness he moves into praise, which is expressed beautifully in the very next chapter, Psalm 8. This psalm is a perfect example of taking negative thoughts captive and moving yourself into a place of hope and faith by being grateful.

In another psalm, we see how gratitude is a gateway.

Enter his gates with thanksgiving and his courts with praise; give thanks to him and praise his name (Psalm 100:4).

One of the most powerful aspects of gratitude is that it can be done out of self-discipline and is not dependent on feelings. In other words, you don't have to feel thankful to be thankful. The beauty of this practice, however, is that once you do it for a while, your feelings begin to explode with praise as you realize how much God has done for you. Even if you feel distant from God, as you begin to express your gratitude you move yourself through a spiritual gate. As your thankfulness turns to praise, you draw nearer still into His courts. When you purposefully turn your praise into worship, you can then enter into the Holy of Holies, into His very presence. Do you see how simple and yet powerful gratitude can turn your heart and change your thoughts from worry to joy?

I have made it a part of my daily meditation to recite the many things in my life for which I am grateful. Because I do this regularly, it has become both natural and easy to do. The gratitude pathway in my brain is frequently used and has become a stronghold for me, a place of power that is difficult for the enemy to scale with discouragement.

What makes you thankful? What provides goodness and blessing in your life? Do you have shelter, food, friends, family, employment, health? Even in the midst of difficult circumstances you can always find something for which to be grateful.

The autobiography written by Corrie Ten Boom demonstrates this principle perfectly.[3] Corrie tells the story of her and her sister being imprisoned in a German concentration camp during World War II for giving refuge to Jews. They were living in deplorable conditions, starving, treated cruelly, and surrounded by death. To top it off, the barracks they had recently moved to were cramped and infested with fleas. Corrie became quite discouraged and found it difficult to be thankful. However, her sister Betsie, who was in much poorer health, insisted that they thank God for their new home. They quickly discovered that the prison guards refused to come into their barracks because of the fleas. This allowed them to have Bible studies and minister to the other women in their barracks without interference. What appeared to be horrible became a blessing to them.

Betsie was able to look at her world and purposefully find something to be thankful for, no matter her circumstances. We too can make gratitude purposeful in our thought life. It is easy to be thankful for the obvious blessings in your life, but what about the blessings that are more hidden? Are you in a difficult situation? What can you find in your situation that makes you thankful? Begin to thank God for that little blessing, hidden in ugliness, and then watch the Lord change your heart from discouragement to joy.

Linda, a patient of mine, was full of anxious thoughts because her adult son was addicted to drugs. She worried that her son would never get over his addiction, and she felt drained from "helping him out" so frequently. So much so that she came in seeking help for her anxiety.

After listening to a litany of complaints, I asked Linda what made her feel thankful. She looked at me blankly, and there was a prolonged pause. I could tell Linda was struggling with this request. Her thought patterns were so dominated by her problems that she had a hard time finding anything good in her life. Finally, Linda began to tell me what made her feel thankful. Her countenance lifted as her thoughts shifted from what was wrong to what was good in her life. In the process of working through her codependency issues and learning how to set healthy boundaries, Linda began to get freedom in other areas of her life. Her relationship with her son eventually improved.

Through involvement in a substance abuse group, Linda became instrumental in helping others, which brought her much joy. Linda told me how thankful she was that God had taken a horrible situation and used it to set her free. If she had not suffered through this adversity, she would never have learned the joy of helping others. Linda had much to be thankful for, and it started in the midst of her trial, not when the trial was over.

As my pastor, Bill Johnson, regularly says, "It doesn't matter the hand you're dealt because God can win with a pair of twos." Paul describes it this way:

> *But thanks be to God, who in Christ always leads us in triumphal procession, and through us spreads the fragrance of the knowledge of him everywhere* (2 Corinthians 2:14 ESV).

When we are facing a crisis, we have an opportunity like no other to be the aroma of Christ to those who are perishing. It is easy to be thankful when things are good, but much more powerful in adversity. Even death itself has been swallowed up in victory. Paul writes:

> *"Where, O death, is your victory? Where, O death, is your sting?"...But thanks be to God! He gives us the victory through our Lord Jesus Christ* (1 Corinthians 15:55,57).

Are you struggling with a terrible situation where there appears to be no hope? Although it sounds strange, there is a place of gratitude even when circumstances are horrific. God is good all of the time, and He only gives us good gifts. He is not the cause of illness or tragedy.

God is always on our side, and He truly loves us and has our best interest at heart. Not everything that happens to us is God's will. When we express gratitude to God in the midst of our trials we can take that which is unclean and make it holy. Gratitude is not only a virtue but a weapon that causes our enemy to fall into a trap set for us.

Our life here on this earth is but a moment in all of eternity, a temporary interim. Our future, our eternity is Heaven. Although we grieve for loved ones who have died, we know we will be with them again. As followers of Jesus, earth is the only hell we will ever know. How can we be threatened by Heaven? I do not deny the process of grief and loss. Jesus Himself wept over the death of Lazarus. However, if you look, you can find a place of thankfulness even while grieving.

The well-loved hymn "It Is Well with My Soul" was written by Horatio Spafford after several tragedies. In 1871, his four-year-old son died, and shortly after that he suffered financial ruin in the great Chicago Fire. He then decided to take his family to England to assist Moody and Sankey in revival meetings. Just before the trip, he was unable to go but sent his family on ahead with plans to come soon after. During the trip, their ship was sunk, and all four of his daughters perished. As he and his wife sailed back over the area where his daughters perished, he penned the lyrics to this amazing hymn:

> *When peace like a river, attendeth my way,*
> *When sorrows like sea billows roll;*
> *Whatever my lot; Thou hast taught me to say,*
> *It is well, it is well, with my soul.*

A few years ago, I cared for a lovely woman who had metastatic cancer. She and her husband had moved to Redding from another state. They had heard the testimonies of healing coming from Bethel Church and they wanted to live in an environment of faith. Although they pursued both prayer and every avenue of treatment offered by our medical community, she died within a year of moving here. I will never forget talking to her husband a few days after she had gone home to be with Jesus. He was full of thankfulness for the care we had provided medically and the love and prayers of the church. He told me that even in his wife's death he had a deep-seated joy in his heart because he knew his wife was no longer suffering. Although he loved and missed his wife, he had determined that he would not question or be angry with God. He was so thankful that they had moved here and that she was able to live her last days in a hopeful environment. Then he shared how the Lord had gifted him with joy and peace in the midst of his sorrow. In all of my years of practice, I had never seen such a healthy approach taken to such a devastating loss.

Unfortunately, our culture views death as an enemy that must be fought to the bitter end. In general, we do not have a society that copes with death in a healthy manner; in fact, we have grief support groups that help people through the process. The Lord, however, has promised us thankfulness and victory even in death.

If you struggle with thankfulness and need some fresh ideas, read Psalm 136. David starts this psalm by declaring:

> *Give thanks to the Lord, for he is good. His love endures forever* (Psalm 136:1).

Then David makes a statement about who God is and follows it with *His love endures forever.* This entire chapter is full of statements of thanksgiving and declarations of God's love. Just reading this psalm makes me feel happy and full of faith.

Rejoicing and giving thanks in all circumstances gives us access to peace and protects our soul and our spirit. While imprisoned, Paul wrote to the Philippians and told them to rejoice in the Lord always and to be anxious about nothing. He instructed them to present their requests to God by prayer and with thanksgiving and then the peace of God, which transcends all understanding, would guard their hearts and minds (see Phil. 4:4-7). Later in this chapter, he described how he had learned the secret of being content in every situation.

I want to comprehend and learn that secret, don't you? I want to be able to sleep in the midst of the storm like Jesus. I want to be able to sing hymns after being beaten and put in stocks in prison like Peter and Silas. And I want to find reasons to be thankful for "pests" in my life that make me feel unclean like Betsie Ten Boom.

GENEROSITY

A related companion to gratitude is generosity. These two attributes are typically found together because generosity is the natural outflow of gratitude. Generosity is the act of giving to others without expecting anything in return and includes financial aid, time, talents, effort, love, forgiveness, praise, encouragement, or other resources.

It is in our best interest to be generous. Jesus Himself said:

Give, and it will be given to you. A good measure, pressed down, shaken together and running over, will be poured into your lap. For with the measure you use, it will be measured to you (Luke 6:38).

We all want to receive, but some of us struggle with the giving part. If you're not receiving much, you might want to evaluate your generosity.

This familiar verse is frequently used as a text to support our financial responsibilities in tithing or some other charitable activity, and rightfully so. However, there is a much larger context here. Jesus was preaching to a crowd of followers, and prior to the comment above He told them that they were blessed if they were poor, hungry, weepy, hated, and rejected. Then He told them to rejoice and leap for joy. Can't you just imagine the looks of confusion on the faces of His followers as they tried to connect rejoicing with being poor? I doubt many people were jumping for joy. Jesus went on to preach about *giving* by loving your enemies, blessing those who curse you, giving to everyone who asks, being merciful, not judging, and forgiving others.

The generosity Jesus speaks of is a generosity of our heart, our speech, and our actions. Jesus understood the link between giving and rejoicing. Generosity is good for you. It makes you happy, which is why Solomon wrote:

A generous person will prosper; whoever refreshes others will be refreshed (Proverbs 11:25).

Paul said:

Remember this: Whoever sows sparingly will also reap sparingly, and whoever sows generously will also reap generously (2 Corinthians 9:6).

The root word of generosity is *generosus*, and it comes from the same Latin word that speaks of noble birth. There is an element of nobility or royalty to generosity. We understand that God gave His only Son for us and that we are joint heirs with Christ. When we understand our position in Christ, we realize how much we've been given and forgiven. The natural response to this generosity is to be grateful and to express this gratitude through a lifestyle of generosity.

Grateful people understand how the generosity of others affects their life. Gratitude has a compelling force to it, an obligation to pass it forward by being generous with others.

People involved with helping others with their time, efforts, or resources are more fulfilled compared to those who do not give to others. Research studies show that individuals who volunteer regularly score higher in levels of satisfaction compared to nonvolunteers.[4]

There is a chemical reaction that occurs within our brains when we are generous to others. Researchers working on the *Cognitive and Emotional Health Project: The Healthy Brain* found that people who donated money had activation of dopamine pathways in their brain.[5] The dopamine pathway is the reward center of the brain, and it is activated by sex, food, money, and drugs. In other words, giving makes you feel good.

Why Good Things Happen to Good People, written by Stephen Post and Jill Neimark, is a compilation of research data that shows the positive effects of altruism to both physical and mental health. These authors conclude that generosity reduces depression and the risk of suicide in teens. They also found that volunteerism in older adults reduced mortality and altruism helped people forgive.

It truly is *more blessed to give than to receive.* Generosity is good for your physical, mental, and spiritual health.

ACTION POINTS

1. What are you grateful for?

2. Where are the areas in your life that you have had difficulty finding peace and contentment?

3. In the midst of your trial, what can you thank God for?

4. How could you be more generous with your time, talents, resources, praise, love, and forgiveness?

_____

_____

_____

_____

_____

_____

_____

MEDITATION SCRIPTURES

- Psalm 7
- Psalm 100
- Psalm 136
- 1 Corinthians 15:55,57
- 2 Corinthians 2:14
- 1 Timothy 4:1-5
- Philippians 4
- Luke 6:38
- Acts 20:35
- Proverbs 11:25
- 2 Corinthians 9:6

NOTES

1. Bill and Beni Johnson, *Spiritual Java* (Shippensburg, PA: Destiny Image Publishers, 2010).

2. Robert A. Emmons and Michael E. McCullough, "Counting Blessings versus Burdens: An Experimental Investigation of Gratitude and Subjective Well-being in Daily Life," *Journal of Personality & Social Psychology* 84, no. 2 (2003): 377-89, doi:10.1037//0022-3514.84.2.377.

3. Corrie Ten Boom, *The Hiding Place* (Washington Depot, CT: Chosen Books, 1971).

4. Stephan Meier and Alois Stutzer, "Is Volunteering Rewarding in Itself?" *Economica*, 75, no. 297 (2007): 39-59, doi:10.1111/j.1468-0335.2007.00597.x.

5. Moll et al., "Human Fronto-mesolimbic Networks Guide Decisions about Charitable Donation," *Proceedings of the National Academy of Sciences* 103, no. 42 (2006): 15623-5628, doi:10.1073/pnas.0604475103.

Chapter 15

Worship and Praise

*"God gave worship so that we may become
partners in His highest purposes."*
—Jack Hayford

O f all of the spiritual tools we have at our disposal, I believe worship
and praise are the most powerful. I placed this chapter at the end as
it is the natural progression to remember—give thanks and then worship
God. Worship is what takes us into the presence of God where our mind
is transformed, and worship is our highest calling. We were created for
worship. In fact, we all worship something, whether it is God, recognition,
pleasure, money, power, family, ourselves, or something else. Our first and
highest calling is to worship God, no matter our age, gender, culture, or
occupation. All of creation was designed to worship the creator, and God
himself is looking for true worshipers.

> *But the hour is coming, and is now here, when the true worshipers will worship the Father in spirit and truth, for the Father is seeking such people to worship him. God is spirit, and those who worship him must worship in spirit and truth* (John 4:23-24 ESV).

It's not that God needs our worship. He's not some ego maniac sitting on a throne, needing to be continually reminded of His greatness. I am sure that God is quite confident in His identity. Worship is actually meant for *our* benefit.

Did you know that you worship what you trust? One of my patients, Mark, is in his 60s and is quite wealthy. Mark grew up in a family that was poor. His mother died of an illness when he was quite young because his family could not afford the needed medical care. This loss caused Mark to determine that when he grew up he would never allow himself to be poor. Mark pursued an education and was able to get a scholarship to a well-known university. His drive and intelligence resulted in a string of business successes and great wealth. Unfortunately, this drive for riches consumed his time and energies, leaving little time for his family. The result was two failed marriages and estrangement from his children. Mark's trust in riches as a response to a fear of poverty caused him to idolize wealth. Do you put your trust in something other than God out of fear? If so, that will become an idol or a place of worship for you.

This principle is the reason Solomon, the wisest man in all of history, said:

> *The fear of the Lord is the beginning of knowledge, but fools despise wisdom and instruction* (Proverbs 1:7).

The fear of the Lord is a wonderful blessing meant to bring you knowledge, wisdom, and discipline for a healthy life. A proper fear of the Lord drives out lesser fears.

How great is your goodness, which You have stored up for those who fear You (Psalm 31:19 NASB).

The fear of the Lord is a deep reverence for the nature of God. When we correctly fear the Lord, we understand that His glory and majesty are indescribable and that every breath comes from Him. Although He is holy and perfect, we are welcomed into His presence because of what Christ has done for us. When we fear God, we desire to please Him above all, and this drives out all other options. To correctly fear God is to know Him, and this is why the fear of the Lord is the beginning of wisdom. If we do not fear God, we do not know Him. To know God is to trust God, and when we trust Him, we *worship Him in spirit and truth.*

Worship is an expression of value or worth, and it is the result of a thankful heart that recognizes the nature of God. I know people who are thankful and do not worship God, but I know of no worshipers who are not thankful. Thanksgiving is critical because it is the seed for praise and worship. If you struggle giving praise and worship to God, check your level of appreciation.

Enter into his gates with thanksgiving, and into his courts with praise: be thankful unto him, and bless his name (Psalm 100:4 KJV).

Gratitude allows us to enter the outer gates. When we are thankful, we recognize what God has done for us—perhaps the beauty of a sunset, protection from injury in a serious accident, or provision for financial need. Thankfulness causes us to meditate on the goodness of God, which then in turn brings forth praise. Praise is our physical expression of the attributes of God and can be manifested in a variety of forms—speaking, shouting, singing, dancing, lifting hands, playing instruments, and all types of artistic expression.

Give praise to the Lord, proclaim his name; make known among the nations what he has done. Sing to him, sing praise to him; tell of all his wonderful acts (Psalm 105:1-2).

Praise is what moves us from the outer gates into the courts, closer yet to His presence. Both thanksgiving and praise are sacrifices that we give to God.

Through Jesus, therefore, let us continually offer to God a sacrifice of praise—the fruit of lips that openly profess his name (Hebrews 13:15).

Worship, however, is deeper still. In worship, as Bill Johnson says, *you become the sacrifice*. Worship is a response in our hearts that says we see the beauty and wonder of who He is, and we give Him our body, mind, and spirit. Worship is what takes us from the courts of praise into the Holy of Holies, His very presence. This is the place where the mind is renewed.

Therefore, I urge you, brothers and sisters, in view of God's mercy, to offer your bodies as a living sacrifice, holy and pleasing to God—this is your true and proper worship. Do not conform to the pattern of this world, but be transformed by the renewing of your mind. Then you will be able to test and approve what God's will is—his good, pleasing and perfect will (Romans 12:1-2).

Can you see the progression? We start with being thankful. Gratitude helps us focus on what God has done for us. As we see His goodness, our minds and lips explode with praise. Praise propels us closer still to behold Him. As we behold Him, we cannot help but worship Him.

David was a master at using this technique when he was depressed. If you study the Psalms, you will see that David often starts a psalm with his grievances and "feelings." He frequently describes himself as weary, weak, or rejected.

My bones burn like glowing embers. My heart is blighted and withered like grass...In my distress I groan aloud and am reduced to skin and bones (Psalm 102:3-5).

I appreciate David's honesty with God. He was not afraid to tell God how he felt. However, David did not allow his feelings to cloud the greater truth of God's love, mercy, provision, and salvation. A little further David says:

But you, O Lord, sit enthroned forever; your renown endures through all generations (Psalm 102:12).

David had the ability to grab his soul by the lapels and tell his soul what to speak and think.

Why, my soul, are you downcast? Why so disturbed within me? Put your hope in God, for I will yet praise him, my Savior and my God (Psalm 42:5).

This psalm is a beautiful example of David using his spirit to tell his soul what to think and speak. In other words, David's spirit led his soul (mind). Most people I know who suffer from depression are frequently led by their soul, and therein lies the problem. The soul is a better follower than a leader. If your feelings overwhelm you, focus your attention away from your problems and turn it to the nature of God. Put your spirit in control to tell your soul what to think until your feelings come into proper alignment.

God is worthy of praise whether we feel like giving it to Him or not. This truth is much larger than the facts of our circumstances. Turning our attention away from our problems and worries and forcing ourselves to praise God when it's the last thing we *feel* like doing is not easy, which is why it's a sacrifice. Thanksgiving and praise may initially be disciplines—things we do in spite of how we feel. However, the more we do them, the easier they become. So much so that they become ingrained in our thought patterns and can be used instinctively.

My pastor, Bill Johnson, frequently says, "You always become like what you worship." This is the very reason our utmost purpose is to worship God. The more we behold Him, the more we become like Him. What could be better? It's a great trade. We come to Him with all of our stuff and exchange it for His mind on things. God is not anxious, fearful, worried, angry, or sad. Worship transforms us by renewing our minds to the mind of Christ. This is the reason God wants us to worship Him. It's meant to benefit *us*.

> And we all, who with unveiled faces contemplate the Lord's glory, are being transformed into his image with ever-increasing glory, which comes from the Lord, who is the Spirit (2 Corinthians 3:18).

Worship and praise are a lifestyle, not just something we do on Sunday. Our bodies become a continual living sacrifice being offered up to God. When I place my hand on a patient's shoulder in compassion after listening to a sad story of loss, this becomes worship. When I am tired and go the extra mile to research a patient's extensive medical record and call specialists to get help for a patient who has not been properly worked up, this is worship. When I get home late from work, tired, ready to relax and discover instead that I need to fix dinner and do laundry and do so willingly, this too is worship. We can worship God as frequently as we choose to do so. For me, it's often pausing for a moment to turn my attention toward Him and just adore Him for who He is.

The New Testament root word for worship means "to kiss." To worship *in spirit and truth* becomes as intimate as kissing God. When you kiss someone, you must draw very close to them, so close that you physically touch. This is the kind of intimacy that God wants to have with us.

I will extol the Lord at all times; his praise will always be on my lips. ...Those who look to him are radiant; their faces are never covered with shame. This poor man called, and the Lord heard him; he saved him out of all his troubles. The angel of the Lord encamps around those who fear him, and he delivers them. Taste and see that the Lord is good; blessed is the one who takes refuge in him. Fear the Lord, you his holy people, for those who fear him lack nothing (Psalm 34:1,5-9).

Where do you think David received such revelation from God? Revelation comes from intimacy, and intimacy is the byproduct of worship. When you worship, you enter into that special Holy of Holies place—His very presence. This is the place where you discover how much you are accepted and loved. This is the place where lies are replaced with truth and where you find your destiny and purpose. I refer my patients to counseling as I have a tremendous value for counseling. There are some things we need to process and work through with the help of others. But a moment in the presence of God can do what years of counseling may never be able to accomplish, and that is transform your mind into the image of Christ.

I had an experience in worship that forever changed how I viewed Father God, and this experience could never have come through counseling. In my prayer time, I often find myself in a garden where I meet with Jesus. This garden has the appearance of a jungle, which at first was a surprise to me as I tend to like well-manicured gardens. Along one of the paths is a hewn out log where I often sit and talk to Jesus. One day we were strolling in the garden, and I asked Jesus to take me to the Father. He took me down a path where at the end there was a little rickety wooden gate. As we passed through the gate, I was blinded by an intense light that glowed brilliantly from the top of a hill in front of us. I fell on my face with a sense of paralyzing fear. The thought of going any further was unimaginable. Jesus helped me up, and as He did I caught a glimpse of the outline of a large castle at the top of the hill. There was no living thing on the hill, just an intense golden light. The light was so painful that I buried my head into Jesus' chest, and He put His arm around me. We slowly ascended the hill, and I knew then the meaning of that Scripture about being "hidden in Christ."

I was both frightened and overwhelmed by the holiness of the light. As we got to the front door of the castle, the light dimmed a bit, and I could see an old man standing by the door to let us in. He was slight and somewhat grizzled in appearance, and he wore a flannel shirt with jeans and suspenders. At first I thought he must be the gardener. As we approached, I could see the delight on His face at our visit. He opened the large door, and as we entered I turned to Him. He stretched out His arms and swung me around like you might a small child. At this moment I realized this was the Father, so delighted to see me. He had stopped everything else and was waiting at the door, just like I do when someone I love is coming. He could have come as the Almighty, sitting on a throne, but he came as a simple gardener, unassuming and approachable. The beauty and the intimacy of that moment forever transformed how I view the Father. Yes, He is holy, blindingly so. Yet He sees me through Jesus, and He loves me like no other. He is looking for me, waiting for me to visit him. He is always approachable to me, and I know He's expectantly waiting for me. This revelation came through worship and was meant to bless me and transform my mind into the image of Christ. I never doubt His love and acceptance of me because of this encounter.

To the degree we spend time in His presence, we are transformed into His likeness. I know patients who have been followers of Jesus for many years and have very little transformation into the image of Christ. I also know people who've only known Jesus a short period but have spent a great deal of that time in the Presence. These young believers are light years ahead of the others in their walk with Christ because of the degree of renewal in their minds. Of all of the keys that are mentioned in this book, I believe that both worship and meditation on the word of God are the most important. The purpose of the Word is to help you to know God and to lead you into an encounter with Him. Worship is what brings you into His presence where revelation transforms how you think.

If worship is a weak area for you, read the Psalms aloud until praise fills your heart and mouth. I have not discussed music, but music is a powerful tool that can bypass our soul and minister to our spirit. One of the quickest ways you can turn an anxious heart into a heart of praise is to turn on music and sing your praises to God. If you struggle with worship, surround yourself with worship music.

There is much more that can be said about praise and worship, but I cannot emphasize enough how this tool will transform your mind like no other. Make sure that worship is part of your lifestyle every day.

ACTION POINTS

1. Where do you place your trust? Is this a place of worship for you?

_____

_____

_____

_____

2. If you placed your trust in something other than God in the question above, can you see how this has become a place of worship for you? Ask the Lord to show you the root of the lie, repent and replace the lie with truth.

_____

_____

_____

_____

_____

3. Do you struggle with thankfulness and gratitude? If so, read the previous chapter, then come back and reread this chapter.

4. What are you thankful for?

_____

_____

_____

_____

_____

5. Give praise to God with physical expression—shouting, singing, speaking, dancing, playing an instrument, etc. An example might be, "God, I praise your name because of your great kindness and mercy toward me. You are worthy of all of my praise and adoration. There is none like you." Continue doing this until your spirit takes charge over your soul. Feel free to turn on music.

6. As you praise God and your mind is overwhelmed with His goodness, offer yourself as a living sacrifice to Him. This is the place of worship, encounter, and revelation. Spend as much time as you can in this place and go to it frequently.

> *"Remember that worship is not a*
> *means to an end, it is the end."*
> —BILL JOHNSON.

Chapter 16

Diet and Supplements

*"Let your food be your medicine and
your medicine be your food."*
—HIPPOCRATES

This is the last of three chapters that will deal with methods oriented around the physical treatment of anxiety and depression. How we care for our physical body has a significant effect on our brain, and this area is often neglected. Our body is the temple of the Holy Spirit, and many treat their body poorly and this affects mental functioning. It is so important to remember that the brain is a physical organ that needs proper nutrition, sleep, and exercise. God expects us to steward our body well to carry out His purposes. I have numerous patients who can control their anxiety and depression with proper lifestyle, and this is foundational.

Attempting to treat a poorly cared for physical body with medication and counseling will have limited benefit.

I am often asked if there a special diet or supplements that can be used instead of medication to treat mood disorders. The answer, based on scientific evidence, is *maybe*—not exactly the most desirable response. My task, however, is to present the evidence, not hearsay based on the testimony of friends and family, promotional advertisements, Internet blogs, or a sales pitch by staff at the local health food store. Before we discuss specific nutritional and supplement recommendations that have been shown to be helpful, I want to make a case for evidence-based research. I find so many confused people pulled in every direction by reports in the media, testimonies from friends, and marketing for hundreds of supposedly superior, organic, natural, you-fill-in-the-blank products. Actually, it's not that difficult. We were designed to get what we need from food. The animal kingdom does not take juice, take vitamins, worry about yeast, or perform colon cleanses. We need to get back to basics and limit our exposure to the multi billion dollar supplement aisles.

We are bombarded with information every day. How do we *"Prove all things; hold fast that which is good"* as Paul instructed the church in Thessalonica? (1 Thess. 5:21 KJV). I find this challenging, even as a medical provider. It is not uncommon for me to receive one or two medical journals daily. Somehow in my busy day I need to review the latest research so that I can stay current and relevant to my patients. Medicine is a very fluid field, and new diagnostic testing, treatment recommendations, surgical procedures, and medications are put into practice on a regular basis. Numerous research studies are done every year, and the results of these studies compel us to change our practice.

What can be more confusing is that the experts are often conflicted. One day a report states caffeine is detrimental to your health, and the next day you see a study that shows drinking one or two cups of coffee daily may be beneficial. Which report do you believe? This is a valid question that deserves an answer. The questions we should be asking are "What is the evidence or proof this treatment works?" and "How safe is this product or procedure?"

Before we discuss specific nutritional and supplement therapies, I'd like to present a brief overview of evidence-based health care. Although the terms *complementary* and *alternative medicine* are quite popular, I believe these terms are misleading. There are only three possibilities in medicine (whether conventional, alternative, or complementary). Either the treatment or medicine has been proven to work, proven not to work, or is unproven or unknown.

I like this quote:

> "There cannot be two kinds of medicine—conventional and alternative. There is only medicine that has been adequately tested and medicine that has not, medicine that works and medicine that may or may not work. Once a treatment has been tested rigorously, it no longer matters whether it was considered alternative at the outset. If it is found to be reasonably safe and effective, it will be accepted."[1]

Unfortunately, the focus of importance for many people has become the origin of the treatment instead of proof that the product is safe and effective. A product that is natural like tobacco, marijuana, opium, etc. is not necessarily safe. On the other hand, God has blessed us with a variety of plants and minerals that do provide legitimate treatment alternatives for certain conditions. Many of these products are safe and effective, and I am going to talk about a few of them here with respect to mood disorders. Let me also make the point that many of the medications we prescribe are derived from certain compounds found in plants. And all medications, whether plant based or artificially created, are derived from products that God created for our benefit. Again, the appropriate question is not about the origin of the treatment, but does this treatment work and is it safe?

The supplement industry is not regulated similarly to the pharmaceutical industry. For a medication to be approved by the FDA (Federal Drug Administration) the medication must meet extremely rigorous standards for both safety and efficacy. Companies that make pharmaceuticals are also monitored closely for the purity of their product. In other words, if your medication label states that there are 50 milligrams in each tablet, there really are 50 milligrams of the active product in each tablet. Prescription medications are not without risks, but the majority of the risks are known. If I understand that a patient is taking a particular medication, I then know what other medications or supplements may interact with that medication, and I know what side effects or laboratory tests I need to monitor. The same cannot be said for many supplements. In essence, a company that produces supplements does not need to prove that their product effectively treats any particular condition, nor that their product is safe or pure. Only when a product is shown to cause substantial harm (an example would be ephedra) does the FDA step in and remove the product from the market.

Certainly, prescription medications have subsequently been pulled from shelves after being found harmful. For this reason, I rarely prescribe medications that are newly released. A research trial may have several thousand subjects in their study. But when a medication is released into the market and hundreds of thousands of people are taking the drug, some uncommon but dangerous side effects may occur. For every medication that is approved by the FDA, there are hundreds of others that are rejected. Scientific research isn't perfect, but it is the best method we have. If randomized, placebo-controlled, double-blinded studies mandated for pharmaceuticals were applied to the supplement industry, there would be a lot of empty shelves!

Another area of grave concern with supplements is multiple ingredients and contamination. When a supplement has a proprietary blend of numerous ingredients, the risk for interaction with other supplements or medications begins to increase. I am stunned by the number of patients who bring in a large bag of supplements that their family, friend, or coworker has recommended to them. As I review the labeling on the products, I often find a great deal of duplications and proprietary blending. People incorrectly assume that if the product is natural and does not require a prescription, then the product is safe.

Unfortunately, this is just not true. One day a patient came into my office complaining of general malaise, fatigue, and nausea. Laboratory testing showed extremely high liver enzymes. She was not taking any prescription medication that could have caused liver inflammation; she did not drink alcohol, and other causes of liver disease were ruled out. Her condition did not make sense. Finally, I asked her about supplements, and she admitted to taking several. She brought them in, and as I looked at the list of ingredients, I realized she was duplicating several herbal products that had the potential for interaction and liver damage. I had her stop all of the supplements and within a short period her liver enzymes returned to normal and her symptoms resolved.

The *New England Journal of Medicine* published an article by Pieter Cohen, MD of Harvard Medical School that reported an alarming number and variety of supplements are contaminated with toxic plant material, heavy metals, bacteria, prescription medications, controlled substances, and experimental compounds or drugs rejected by the FDA because of safety concerns.[2] Obviously, nobody wants to take a product that would make them ill. Our bodies are the temple of the Holy Spirit, and Paul instructs us in to honor God with our body (see 1 Cor. 6:20). For this reason, the scientific method, which is the foundation of evidence-based medicine, is the closest thing we have to "Prove all things and hold to that which is good."

So how can you get accurate information about a supplement? I recommend Consumer Laboratory at www.consumerlab.com, which is a company that independently tests supplements for accuracy and contamination, and the National Center for Complementary and Alternative Medicine at http://nccam.nih.gov/health/supplements for unbiased and scientific information about specific supplements. Another simple way to make sure you are buying a product that has been tested for quality, purity, and potency is to look for the USP (United States Pharmacopeia) logo on the label. USP is a nonprofit scientific organization that certifies supplements to a very high standard. Look for this logo on the label:

Remember that the supplement market is a multibillion dollar industry and much of the information on the Internet is promotional in nature and designed to separate you from the dollars in your pocket. A product that is purported to treat numerous conditions should be viewed with a great deal of skepticism. Just because the promotional literature states *research shows* or *scientific evidence demonstrates* that this supplement *supports* or *assists* brain health does not make it so.

Sadly, I find many Christians are coaxed into buying expensive supplements by other Christians, particularly by those people who are held in high esteem. Although intentional fraud does occur, I believe that most of the time people are captured by the power of the testimony. Testimony to the acts of God is a powerful tool to build faith. When we hear what God has done for others, we can believe He will do the same for us. However, testimonials and anecdotal evidence are only starting points for true scientific research. Yet testimonials are often the "research or evidence" touted by the supplement industry. What you want to ask about any product is has this product been tested in a randomized (selected by a randomized computer program to remove bias), double-blinded (neither the subject nor researcher knows which product is being used), placebo-controlled study (the product is being tested against a group that is receiving an identical sugar pill)?

Some other points to consider when evaluating research are to look at the number of subjects in the study. A study of twenty people has very little validity compared to a study of one thousand people. Valid scientific studies are repeatable. If I see that that there are three or more studies drawing the same conclusion about a product, then I have a great deal of more confidence about that product. Repeatability is an area that trips people up. Many manufacturers will promote *scientific evidence-based* on one small study in support of their product, ignoring other studies of their product that show no benefit.

The last point I want to make before I discuss specific nutritional recommendations is that a product needs to be tested in humans. I know this sounds silly, but just because a product shows promise in the laboratory or works in rats doesn't mean it works in humans. Many of the *scientific evidence* claims in the supplement industry are based on laboratory testing. Unfortunately what works in the lab may not work in the human body. I highly recommend *Alternative Medicine: The Christian Handbook* written by Donal O'Mathuna, Ph.D. and Walt Larimore, MD for a comprehensive analysis of evidence-based medicine and alternative medicine. This book is an excellent resource for showing, which treatments have a valid benefit and those that have no benefit or may be harmful.

DIET AND NUTRITION

So back to the question—are there specific dietary recommendations for people who suffer from anxiety and depression? Yes, and these are the same heart-healthy recommendations that everyone on the planet should be following. If you think about it, Jesus modeled the perfect lifestyle for us. We tend to focus on what Jesus said or the acts He performed, but what about the way He lived? His diet consisted of whole grains, legumes, fruits, vegetables, olive oil, eggs, dairy, and fish or poultry. Red meat would have been an expensive luxury and not a usual part of the diet in that region. Sweets would have been minimal—fruits, dates, and occasionally honey. Much of what we eat today—think of processed foods in a package—would have been completely foreign to Jesus. In addition to eating a healthy diet, Jesus got plenty of sunshine and extensive exercise, something most Americans avoid.

Although I don't have proof, I suspect Jesus had a normal BMI (body mass index). Obesity would have been unusual in His society, which cannot be said for most cities in the United States today. America and much of the Western world is facing an epidemic of obesity. The effects of obesity on the health care system for the next 30 years will be staggering. Obesity is a major player in coronary artery disease, hypertension, diabetes, and cancer, the major causes of morbidity and mortality. What most people don't realize is that obesity is also a risk factor for depression.

Interestingly enough, the foods that Jesus ate are what we now call the Mediterranean diet. Numerous scientific studies have shown that people who eat a Mediterranean diet live longer and have less cardiovascular disease, cancer, obesity, diabetes, Alzheimer's, dementia, and depression compared to other groups.

A recent article published by the *American Journal of Psychiatry* showed that people who consumed a diet high in vegetables, fruit, fish, nuts, whole grains, and olive oil were 30 percent less likely to develop depression than people who consumed a diet high in processed meats, refined grains, sugars, fried foods, and high-fat dairy.[3] It is speculated that the higher levels of antioxidants and omega-3 fats found in the Mediterranean diet are protective to the brain and vascular system as opposed to the negative inflammatory effects of a diet high in processed foods.

Processed foods are often loaded with corn syrup and other sugars that have a high glycemic index. When ingested these foods cause a rapid rise in blood sugar. In response to the rush of sugar into the bloodstream, the pancreas is forced to release a bolus of insulin to lower the blood sugar. These swings in blood sugar will often cause fatigue, irritability, and mental "fogginess," none of which are helpful for someone struggling with anxiety or depression.

One day, a gentleman came into the office seeking treatment for anxiety that he had been struggling with for several years. He noticed that if he ate any dessert or sugary drink his heart would begin to race, he would feel anxious and then become dizzy. After we had done some laboratory testing, we found he had an allergy to cane sugar. This allergic reaction caused activation of the fight–flight pathway in his brain, resulting in adrenaline being released into his bloodstream. The adrenaline rush stimulated a panic attack. As you can imagine, he became quite motivated to look at the ingredient list on the label of any food he bought so as to avoid cane sugar and corn syrup!

So what is the Mediterranean diet? The foundation of the Mediterranean diet food pyramid is fruits, vegetables, whole grains, legumes, beans, nuts, seeds, olive oil, and herbs. Some of the foods that have the highest level of antioxidants and are excellent for the brain include berries (particularly blueberries), citrus, stone fruits (cherries, peaches, and plums), kiwis, red grapes, Brussels sprouts, broccoli, beets, cauliflower, spinach and other dark green vegetables, tomatoes, peppers (red or yellow are better), hard squashes, yams, beans, lentils, garbanzo beans, and oats (whole, not instant) just to name a few. Certainly you can eat other fruits and vegetables as well, but if you are struggling with a mood disorder, I would recommend you incorporate some of the below-listed foods as well.

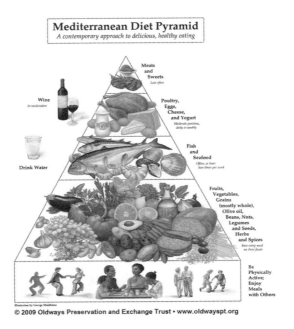

Mediterranean Diet Pyramid
A contemporary approach to delicious, healthy eating

Meats and Sweets
Less often

Wine
In moderation

Poultry, Eggs, Cheese, and Yogurt
Moderate portions, daily to weekly

Drink Water

Fish and Seafood
Often, at least two times per week

Fruits, Vegetables, Grains (mostly whole), Olive oil, Beans, Nuts, Legumes and Seeds, Herbs and Spices
Base every meal on these foods

Be Physically Active; Enjoy Meals with Others

Illustration by George Middleton

© 2009 Oldways Preservation and Exchange Trust • www.oldwayspt.org

Try to eat six to eight servings of fruits and vegetables each day and eat from the rainbow. In other words, choose fruits and vegetables with a variety of colors and eat them raw or slightly undercooked when possible. Make sure the bread you eat is whole grain and high in fiber. Dip your bread in olive oil instead of spreading it with butter and use olive oil or canola oil for cooking instead of hydrogenated fats. Choose whole grains like bulgur, brown rice, quinoa, and whole wheat pasta instead of regular pasta and white rice. Whole grains have more fiber and a lower glycemic index compared to refined grains. Foods that are converted into glucose more slowly allow our pancreas to keep insulin and glucose levels more even. Preventing a rapid rise and drop in blood glucose makes for a much happier and higher functioning brain. Avoid skipping meals as this causes low blood glucose levels leading to irritability, moodiness, and carbohydrate craving.

Nuts and seeds are also a healthy part of the Mediterranean diet as they are high in protein and monounsaturated fats. Almonds, cashews, walnuts, and pistachios make great snacks. A word of caution with nuts— as they are high in calories, limit your intake to a small handful daily if losing weight is a struggle for you. Tahini (sesame seed spread), almond butter, and natural peanut butter are also good choices. Make sure that you check the label on these nut spreads as some of them have added sugar and sodium that makes them poor choices.

Use herbs and spices to season your food instead of salt. Sodium intake should not exceed 2,000 milligrams daily. Seventy percent of the sodium in your diet is hidden in your food and not from sprinkling salt on your food. Many of my patients are convinced they are on a low sodium diet because they never salt their food. But as I review their actual dietary intake with them they usually exceed the recommended 2,000 milligrams daily. Obesity and the high sodium intake of most Americans are leading causes of hypertension, resulting in heart disease, stroke, and kidney failure. Cardiovascular disease is the leading cause of death in the United States, and hypertension is the number one culprit.

The second level in the Mediterranean diet pyramid is fish and seafood. Very few of my patients eat seafood on a regular basis. Unfortunately, fish tends to be costlier than other meats, and many people just don't like fish. Seafood, however, is one of the healthiest meats on our planet as it is loaded with protein and omega-3 fatty acids. Much of our brain is comprised of fat and requires omega-3 fatty acids to function properly. Fish with the largest amount of omega-3 (DHA and EPA) concentrations are found in deep, cold water. These fish include salmon (wild), tuna (fresh), sardines, anchovies, herring, trout, and mackerel. Omega-3 fatty acids are found in other fish and shellfish as well but in lower concentrations. Patients often tell me they don't like fish, so they take flaxseed oil instead. The problem with flaxseed oil is that it is comprised of a different type of omega-3 (ALA) that your body has difficulty converting into DHA.

As some species of fish may be contaminated with mercury or PCBs (large fish that are higher on the food chain, i.e. swordfish and shark) the FDA has recommended limiting seafood intake to two servings or 12 ounces per week. Seafood sources known to be lower in mercury include salmon, canned tuna, shrimp, catfish, and pollock. Obviously, you don't want to negate the health benefits of seafood by frying it, so baking or grilling is preferred.

The third level on the pyramid is poultry, eggs, cheese, and yogurt which should be consumed in moderation. Cheese and ice cream are high in fat and/or sugar. Better choices in this category would be milk, yogurt, eggs, and poultry. There are lower-fat versions for some of these products if weight or elevated cholesterol are an issue for you. Avoid eating the skin of poultry. Other healthy options in this category would be tofu and soy products.

The last category in the Mediterranean diet pyramid is meats and sweets. Limit your intake of red meat to once a week and choose leaner cuts of meat. Avoid sausage and bacon that are high in fat and sodium. Minimize your intake of sweets (this includes sodas and many juices that are high in sugar) and desserts.

Try to drink plenty of water, six to eight glasses per day. Put a slice of lemon or a sprig of mint in your water if you have a hard time drinking water plain. Another option is to brew green tea. Green tea is loaded with antioxidants and may help with weight loss. Although containing up to 40 milligrams of caffeine per cup, green tea also contains theanine, an amino acid that has a calming effect on the brain and is an agonist to caffeine. Caffeine is a stimulant and interferes with normal sleep. Limit your caffeine intake to no more than 300 milligrams daily and avoid caffeine later in the day and evening.

Avoid sugary drinks, sodas, and energy drinks. Many people have adverse reactions to artificial sweeteners, so minimize or avoid these products as well.

Although the Mediterranean diet includes wine in moderation, I strongly recommend that my patients suffering from anxiety or depression avoid alcohol. Alcohol is a depressant and adversely affects neurotransmitters. Even two servings of alcohol per week can negate the effects of antidepressant medications. Alcohol can also aggravate anxiety and interferes with REM sleep. People often use alcohol to "de-stress" and help them sleep. However, the quality of sleep after consuming alcohol is quite poor. Bottom line—avoid alcohol if you struggle with anxiety or depression.

The Mediterranean diet is a heart-healthy diet. And whatever is good for the heart is also good for the brain. Your brain needs optimal blood flow to function correctly. Lack of blood flow to the brain results in areas of brain death, which can contribute to dementia. I have cared for numerous patients who develop profound changes in their personality after suffering a stroke or from developing Alzheimer's dementia. People who were previously happy and stable in their mood become depressed, moody, and anxious. Their family will tell me that they don't even recognize their loved one. It's as if they were dealing with a completely different person. This change can happen when brain neurons die and cells that were formerly able to produce neuroactive chemicals like serotonin and dopamine no longer work. It's important to keep your heart healthy and your arteries open if you want to maintain optimal brain function.

An easy way to approach this diet is first to focus on getting six to eight servings of fruits and vegetables daily. Plan your meals and snacks around fruits and vegetables first, as these are now become your main course instead of meat. Then make sure you have a source of lean protein with each meal, legumes and whole grains or fish being preferred sources of protein. Next incorporate a modest amount of nuts, seeds, and lean dairy or poultry. Meat should be the condiment, not the focus of the meal. If you can do this, you won't have a lot of room left for unhealthy foods. Before you grab a snack, make sure you've had your daily quota of fruits, vegetables, and water. You will find that not only are you less hungry, your mental clarity, energy level, and mood have improved as well.

VITAMINS AND SUPPLEMENTS

So what about taking vitamins and supplements to help anxiety and depression? Is there any scientific evidence that these products are beneficial and safe? The answer is yes, for *some* people. There are no products that work universally for everyone, but there are several vitamins and supplements that may help and are worth a try.

First, let me say that vitamins and supplements cannot make up for a poor diet. Many people would love just to take a vitamin so they don't have to bother with eating fruits and vegetables. The following is a great example of this principle.

Initial studies done many years ago showed that people who ate foods high in antioxidants (fruits and vegetables) had fewer cancers than those individuals who ate diets with low levels of antioxidants. Scientists theorized that Vitamin A, beta carotene, Vitamin E, Vitamin C, and selenium (antioxidants) prevented free radical damage to cells, thus reducing the incidence of cancer. The media reported the finding and supplement industry began to market antioxidant supplements for cancer prevention on the assumption that the antioxidants themselves, not the food, prevented cancer. Unfortunately, you can't get your cancer prevention in a pill. You actually have to eat the foods to get the benefit. A meta-analysis (statistical review of a group of studies) of 68 randomized trials showed that people who took extra beta-carotene, Vitamin A, and Vitamin E (alone or in combination) actually increased their risk of dying compared to a control group.[4] There is something about the balance and ratio of nutrients in the foods we eat that cannot be duplicated in a pill. If you are eating the recommended Mediterranean diet above, you will be getting plenty of antioxidants and don't need to take antioxidant supplements.

That being said, the following is a review of several supplements that may be helpful for anxiety or depression. More is not necessarily better and, in fact, may be harmful, so carefully follow dosing recommendations. Some of these supplements may interact with certain medications, so check with your medical provider if you are taking other medications.

Omega-3 Fish Oil

Omega-3 fatty acids are essential nutrients for cell function and are good polyunsaturated fats naturally found in fish, flaxseed, nuts, soybeans, and avocados. Fish, however, contains DHA and EPA, which is superior to the ALA type of omega-3 found in flaxseed oil and nuts. Our bodies do not make these fatty acids, so we need to incorporate them into our diet. Omega-3 fish oil is thought to be anti-inflammatory, and research suggests that people taking omega-3 fish oil supplements have less cardiovascular disease. Your brain depends on healthy arteries to supply oxygen and nutrients. So anything that is good for your cardiovascular system is good for your brain.

Although results were mixed, there are several clinical studies that suggest omega-3 fish oil may have a beneficial effect for adults with depression and bipolar disorder as a complement to standard care. The clinical guidelines of the Canadian Network for Mood and Anxiety Treatments (CANMAT) list omega-3 fish oil as a second-line adjunctive treatment for major depressive disorder (MDD).[5]

Omega-3 fish oil is well tolerated, with occasional complaints of burping up a fishy taste. If this is bothersome, you can purchase enteric coated capsules that are digested further down in the intestinal tract, store them in the freezer, or take them at bedtime. The recommended dose for treatment of mood disorder is four to six grams daily. Fish oil can affect clotting time, so if you are taking blood thinners such as warfarin or clopidogrel or if you have a bleeding disorder, check with your medical provider before you initiate omega-3 fish oil.

SAM-e

SAM-e (S-adenosylmethionine) is an amino acid produced and used by your brain in several neurotransmitter processes, including the production of dopamine and serotonin. In people who are depressed, SAM-e production can be impaired. Several studies have shown that SAM-e was superior to placebo in helping with mild to moderate depression. CAN-MAT recommends SAM-e as a second-line treatment for mild to moderate MDD.[6] People who have bipolar or manic-depressive disorder should not take SAM-e.

The usual recommended dose of SAM-e for adults is 200 to 400 milligrams twice daily. In some cases, 800 milligrams twice daily can be used, but there may be increased risks of serotonin toxicity with higher doses, particularly if used with other medications that raise serotonin. This condition is quite serious, causing agitation, increased heart rate and blood pressure, fever, sweating, and if untreated can be fatal.

Side effects for SAM-e may include nausea, anxiety, insomnia, dry mouth, headache, and rashes. Consider using SAM-e if you are suffering from depression, as long as you do not have bipolar or manic-depressive disorder. If you are already taking an antidepressant, talk to your medical provider before you start SAM-e.

St. John's Wort

This herbal product is derived from the Hypericum plant and has been proven in clinical trials to be superior to placebo in treating mild to moderate depression, although not as effective in severe depression. The mechanism of action is unclear, but St. John's Wort does affect several neurotransmitter pathways, including those for serotonin, norepinephrine, and gamma aminobutyric acid (GABA).

The recommended dose for treatment of mild to moderate depression is 300 to 600 milligrams twice daily. St. John's Wort is usually well tolerated and was found to have fewer side effects than comparable antidepressant medications. CANMAT recommends St. John's Wort as a first-line treatment for mild to moderate MDD.[7]

St. John's Wort can cause increased photosensitivity and can interact with other medications and with alcohol. This product is metabolized via the cytochrome P450 pathway in your liver, which is the same pathway utilized by many medications. So check with your medical provider before initiating treatment with St. John's Wort.

Vitamin B

The B vitamins play a role in the production of neurotransmitters, and there is some evidence that shows low levels of vitamin B_6, B_{12}, and folate may be linked to cognitive impairment and depression. Individuals who suffer from digestive problems, such as celiac disease or Crohn's disease, those who have had gastric bypass surgery, and the elderly are at increased risk for Vitamin B deficiency. Besides eating a Mediterranean diet, which is high in B vitamins, I recommend taking a B-complex daily for any of my patients suffering from stress or mood disorder as stress can deplete Vitamin B. In particular, I recommend methylated B_{12}. Many people have a genetic deficiency in the MTHFR pathways that prevents absorption of regular B_{12} supplements, and in fact unmethylated B_{12} can make their condition worse as it competes with the methylated B_{12} in their diet. Laboratory testing can be performed to check for this genetic pathway, but just to be safe I recommend methylated B_{12} of at least 1,000 micrograms daily.

Vitamin D

Vitamin D deficiency is fairly prevalent in my patient population, and there is research that shows a correlation between low Vitamin D levels and seasonal affective disorder (SAD). Vitamin D is primarily found in fish and milk, which I find many people consume inadequately. I recommend 2,000 to 5,000 IU daily of Vitamin D_3. More is not necessarily better, and in some cases can be toxic. Vitamin D is a fat soluble vitamin that is stored in the liver. Excessive amounts can cause liver damage, so don't overdo it.

Other Supplements

I will mention 5-Hydroxytryptophan (5-HTP), which is a derivative of the amino acid tryptophan and plays a part in the production of serotonin. Research on the efficacy of tryptophan for the treatment of depression is mixed, and CANMAT reports insufficient evidence in support of tryptophan.[8] However, there are some studies that suggest 5-HTP may be helpful for anxiety, depression, and insomnia. 5-HTP appears to be well tolerated, and the usual dosage is 100 milligrams twice daily. The most common side effects are gastrointestinal. As 5-HTP may increase serotonin, it should be used with caution when taking St. John's Wort, SAM-e, or SSRI medications that increase serotonin. Check with your medical provider before initiating treatment with 5-HTP.

Although large clinical research trials are lacking, there is some evidence that suggests L-theanine, an amino acid found in green tea, may have a calming effect on the brain. L-theanine seems to affect concentrations of dopamine and serotonin and may improve mental alertness. L-theanine is well tolerated, and the usual dose is 100 to 200 milligrams daily. Alternatively, drink two cups of green tea daily.

Another supplement to consider is dehydroepiandrosterone (DHEA), which is a sex hormone produced by the adrenal glands and is a precursor to the production of estrogen and testosterone. Several studies have shown DHEA to be superior to placebo for the treatment of MDD. However, long-term safety is an issue for this supplement, so it is not something I routinely recommend in my practice. Side effects of DHEA may include acne and increased facial hair. Women with polycystic ovarian syndrome, liver disease, diabetes, breast cancer, ovarian cancer, uterine cancer, uterine fibroids, or endometriosis should not take DHEA. Men with liver problems, diabetes, or prostate or testicular cancer should not take DHEA. Check with your medical provider before initiating treatment with DHEA.

Some other supplements that are used for depression include saffron (*Crocus sativus*), gingko biloba, borage, lavender, and roseroot. However, clinical research trials for both efficacy and safety are limited, so I am currently unable to recommend these products.

SUMMARY

In summary, if you or a loved one is suffering from a mood disorder make sure that you are eating correctly. You truly are what you eat. The Mediterranean diet is recommended for numerous health reasons, including brain and cardiovascular health.

Before initiating any therapy, it is prudent to ask about the effectiveness and the safety of the treatment. What is the quality of the research in support of the treatment? Was there more than one randomized, double-blinded, placebo controlled study that showed this product was effective and safe? Get accurate information from independent sources such as Consumer Laboratory and the National Center for Complementary and Alternative Medicine.

Supplements that may be routinely taken for anyone with a mood disorder include omega-3 fish oil, B vitamin complex, and Vitamin D. Additional supplements such as SAM-e, St. John's Wort, 5-HTP, DHEA, and L-theanine may be helpful as well, but check with your medical provider before initiating treatment as some of these products have safety issues or may interact with other medications.

In conclusion, nutrition and supplements can play a critical role for those suffering with anxiety and depression. People with mild mood disorders can often treat their symptoms with lifestyle alone. Others with moderate to severe anxiety and depression should use diet and lifestyle measures as supportive treatment to help counseling and medication be more effective. In the next chapter, we will explore exercise, sleep, and light therapy as we look for more ways to physically support our brain.

Action Points

1. Instead of focusing on what *not* to eat, look at what you need to eat. As you review the Mediterranean diet, think about how and where you can add six to eight servings of fruits and vegetables into your diet every day. Just doing this will eliminate room for unhealthy foods.

2. Are you using all whole grains? The higher the fiber, the lower the glycemic index. Think of using brown rice, wild rice, quinoa, bulgur, flax seed, millet, and oats to name a few. What foods do you need to eliminate from your pantry?

3. Unless you have an allergy, plan to incorporate fish into your diet at least twice a week. There are some amazing ways to cook fish that are delicious and healthy. Avoid using batter and frying.

4. Make sure you are using healthy oils and work on keeping your sodium intake to 2,000 milligrams or less daily.

5. Making dietary changes require planning and strategy. It doesn't just happen. First, eliminate the junk from your fridge and pantry. If it's not there you can't eat it. If all you have are healthy choices, then when you are hungry you will eat something healthy. This is the same

strategy that is used with alcoholics. If it's not there to tempt you, you lessen the chance of drinking.

6.   Lastly, eat foods that are as close to their God-created state as possible, keep it simple, and avoid fads.

Notes

1.   Marcia Angell and Jerome P. Kassirer, "Alternative Medicine—The Risks of Untested and Unregulated Remedies," *New England Journal of Medicine* 339, no. 12 (1998): 839-41, doi:10.1056/nejm199809173391210.

2.   Pieter A. Cohen, "American Roulette—Contaminated Dietary Supplements," *New England Journal of Medicine* 361, no. 16 (2009): 1523-525, doi:10.1056/nejmp0904768.

3.   T.N. Akbaraly et al., "Dietary Pattern and Depressive Symptoms in Middle Age," *The British Journal of Psychiatry* 195, no. 5 (2009): 408-13, doi:10.1192/bjp.bp.108.058925.

4.   Goran Bjelakovic et al., "Mortality in Randomized Trials of Antioxidant Supplements for Primary and Secondary Prevention," *Jama* 297, no. 8 (2007): 842, doi:10.1001/jama.297.8.842.

5.   A.V. Ravindran et al., "Clinical Guidelines for the Management of Adults with Major Depressive Disorder: Section 5: Complementary and Alternative Medicine Treatments," *The Canadian Journal of Psychiatry* 61, no. 9 (2016): 576-87, doi:10.1177/0706743716660290.

6.   Ibid.

7.   Ibid., 560.

8.   Ibid., 559.

Chapter 17

Exercise, Sleep, and Light Therapy

"An early-morning walk is a blessing for the whole day."
— Henry David Thoreau

In the previous chapter, the importance of nutrition and specific supplements to physically support the brain was reviewed. This chapter will discuss the necessity of exercise, sleep, and light therapy for optimal brain cell function.

EXERCISE

The physical and mental effects of exercise cannot be over-emphasized. Of all of the lifestyle changes, this seems to be the one that people struggle with the most. I want to restate that Jesus is perfect theology and He modeled a lifestyle of exercise. He walked for hours every day. Light therapy was not a problem as He spent a great deal of time outdoors. He ate a Mediterranean diet and didn't juice or take supplements. Lastly, He didn't stay up late at night to watch TV or go online to check emails and social media. He went to bed soon after the sun went down, so eight hours or more of sleep would have been standard. These are the simple things that will change your life more than anything else.

Exercise affects more than your muscles and physical fitness. The actual structure, blood flow, and function of your brain are affected by physical activity. Research by Carl Cotman, PhD, neurobiologist at the University of California, Irvine, reveals that exercise increases blood flow to the brain, improves concentration, reduces loss of gray matter (nerve cell death), promotes growth of new nerve cells, strengthens the synapses between nerve cells, and increases brain-derived neurotrophic factor (BDNF), a growth factor that seems to decrease symptoms of depression.[1]

My patients are familiar with the physical benefits of exercise, such as reduction in rates of obesity, hypertension, stroke, heart attack, diabetes, osteoporosis, and cancers of the colon and breast. However, most of my patients don't realize the profound effect that exercise has on the brain. When you exercise you increase the blood flow and, therefore, the oxygen and nutrients to areas deep inside your brain. This increased flow also protects the brain from free radical toxins that develop when you experience stress.

But exercise also has a direct effect on the individual cells in the nervous system. Exercise seems to boost activity in the frontal lobes and hippocampus of the brain and raises the levels of serotonin, dopamine, and norepinephrine—neurotransmitters affecting mood. It also increases BDNF, which seems to help brain cells survive longer, and that may explain why exercise helps cognition and prevents dementia. In a randomized controlled study (RCT) of 202 adults, exercise proved to work just as well as sertraline (anti-depressant medication) in the treatment of MDD.[2]

Data for the long-term benefits of exercise treatment alone on mood is limited, and there are more studies that show the benefit of combining exercise with medication over exercise alone. CANMAT recommends exercise as an adjunct treatment to medication for mild to moderate MDD but not as monotherapy.[3]

Unless there is a specific reason someone cannot exercise, I recommend at least 30 minutes of exercise five to seven times weekly to all of my patients, whether they have a mood disorder or not. You need to exercise a minimum of 30 minutes three times per week to get a benefit, but more is better. To achieve weight loss, you need to exercise 60 minutes, five to seven times per week. Being "active" around the house or "chasing" your kids does not count. You need an aerobic activity that sustains an elevated heart rate for at least 20 minutes at a time to get a cardiovascular benefit. Aerobic activities include brisk walking, jogging, dancing, swimming, biking, basketball, tennis, any other activity that gets your heart rate up.

Exercise needs to become such a part of your lifestyle that you don't debate whether or not you're going to do it each day. You don't think about brushing your teeth because it is just a part of your morning routine, and this is the way it should be with exercise. The investment of 30 minutes every day into the health of your body and mental function will reap tremendous rewards for you, and it will cost you very little.

Some tips that will help you keep on track include making exercise a part of your daily schedule, preferably in the morning. Research shows that people who exercise in the morning are more likely to do so regularly, followed by afternoon, and with evening being least likely. Make it fun and change it up. Find some sport or activity you enjoy. If you get bored, then do something else. You are more likely to stick with exercise if you are having fun. The Wii Fit Nintendo program has a great variety of fun programs that combine fitness, core-strengthening, balance, and coordination activities. Multitask by watching a favorite television program while you use a stepper or a treadmill, or pray while you take a brisk walk or swim laps in your pool. Join a dance class or activity that involves other people. Many of my male patients play basketball, which is a great way to both exercise and socialize. Zumba seems to be a favorite activity of many of my female patients. It seems less like work when you are having fun.

Getting people to exercise is one of the most difficult things I encounter when I try to get people to make lifestyle changes. I've heard all of the excuses, but the bottom line is that we all do what we want to do. If you *want* to exercise, you will find time for it. You find time to do the other things you want to do, so why not exercise? I have several patients who can control their mood disorders with just exercise. It's that powerful.

SLEEP

Chronic sleep deprivation has a profound effect on mood. Unfortunately, most Americans do not get enough sleep. A hundred years ago Americans averaged nine hours of sleep per night. By 1975 that had decreased to seven and a half hours, and currently the average American only gets seven hours of sleep nightly. Modern conveniences such as light, television, and computers allow us to work and play at night, where previous generations went to bed when the sun went down.

The effects of getting less than seven hours of sleep per night mimic accelerated aging and include weight gain, increased insulin resistance (which can lead to diabetes), hypertension, and memory loss. Individuals who get less than six and a half hours of sleep per night have a decreased ability to fight off infection, difficulty coping with stress, difficulty concentrating, decreased alertness, increased clumsiness, and increased anxiety and depression.

In a study of 25,130 adults, researchers found that chronic insomnia increased the risk of developing depression five-fold and increased the risk of developing an anxiety disorder by twenty-fold.[4]

There is a very close link between mood and sleep. Not only does lack of sleep affect mood, but mood itself can cause sleep disruption. The majority of patients who come into my office seeking treatment for mood disorder are suffering from sleep deprivation.

One day Angela came in to see me. I asked her what brought her in, and she burst into tears, saying "This is not like me. I don't know what is wrong with me. I can't concentrate at work, and every little thing makes me irritable." As I began to take a medical history, I quickly realized that Angela was suffering from sleep deprivation due to frequent awakenings from her hot flashes. Angela was 51 years old and had stopped menses about five months prior. She admitted that she could deal with the hot flashes during the day, but she woke up frequently at night, which never allowed her to drop into REM sleep. The disrupted sleep had been going on for several months, and over-the-counter products advertised to help with menopausal changes had not helped her symptoms. Her moods were seriously affecting her work and her relationships at home. Angela was suffering from depression due to a disruption in neurotransmitters from both sleep deprivation and decreased estrogen. Changes in hormones can have a profound effect on mood. After discussing several treatment options, Angela opted for some low-dose hormone replacement therapy. Her mood and sleep pattern returned to normal within two weeks.

This is a clear-cut example of how sleep can affect mood. I also see this pattern in people who do shift work or who work more than 10 hours per day, 24-hour caregivers, mothers with infants, and anyone juggling a lot of hats or burning the candle at both ends. These people just do not get enough sleep and often end up suffering from anxiety or depression.

Other times the reverse is true. One day Randy came in complaining of depression for a year, but worsening in the past month. Randy was 40 years old and denied having depression in the past. However, as I questioned him, it became apparent that he had suffered from intermittent depression throughout most of his adult life. What actually triggered the office visit was insomnia. Randy was struggling with both falling and staying asleep, and this was affecting his work and marriage. The worsening of his depression had caused a disruption in his sleep pattern. As we treated the mood disorder, his sleep patterns returned to normal.

There are potential risks and side effects to medications, so it's always better to use natural methods to sleep. However, it may be difficult to successfully treat the mood disorder if the patient cannot sleep. Insomnia itself can eventually induce psychosis. So if sleep cycles are severely disrupted, I will often prescribe medications to get patients back into a normal sleep pattern. Most of the time we can get people off of sleep medication as mood improves.

Here are some pointers that help promote good sleep habits.

- Keep to a regular sleep schedule. You have an internal clock and circadian rhythm that operates best on a regular sleep routine. Go to bed and get up the same time each day, even on the weekends. Only go to bed when you are sleepy. If you lie in bed and are unable to fall asleep within 30 minutes, get up and go into another room until you get sleepy. Avoid daytime naps.

- Avoid nicotine, alcohol, and caffeine, particularly in the evening. All of these substances can interfere with REM sleep.

- Keep your bedroom dark, quiet, and comfortable. The area in your brain responsible for triggering sleep is highly sensitive to light. If necessary, use black-out curtains. Make sure your room is at a comfortable temperature and that you have a quality mattress and pillow.

- Avoid physical and mental stimulation two hours prior to bedtime. This is not the time to exercise, read or watch thrillers, work on your computer, or surf the 'net. Instead, read or watch something that is soothing or boring. Develop a regular, relaxing routine that you use each night.

- If you cannot fall asleep because you are thinking of all the things you need to do the next day, get up and make a list. This will help clear your mind of clutter.

- Prayer and meditation are both useful tools to calm and soothe the brain and can help initiate sleep.

- Music and sounds can both be used to help initiate sleep. Background instrumental music that is soft and slow, nature sounds, and white noise such as a fan can all be hypnotic and soothing to the brain.

- A warm bath with candlelight and a massage can help induce relaxation. Essential oils used in aromatherapy such as lavender, ylang-ylang, clary sage, sandalwood, chamomile, and geranium are reported to have sedating properties and reduce stress and tension. Although there is little clinical research to verify the effectiveness of these oils, some studies show benefit and the cost and risks of treatment are minimal. Make sure you use aromatherapy oils as recommended as they are quite concentrated and avoid them if you develop any adverse reactions.[5]

- Don't use your bed for anything but sleep and sex. All other activities such as computer work, eating, and watching television should be done in another room.

- Avoid eating a heavy meal or drinking a lot of fluids before bedtime.

- Avoid sleeping with your children or pets as their movements may awaken you in the night.

- If you are taking medications, review possible side effects that may be interfering with your sleep pattern.

- If you have tried all of the above and are still struggling with falling or staying asleep, talk to your medical provider about other treatments for your sleep disorder.

Sleep apnea is a common disorder that can be very disruptive to normal sleep cycles. This condition occurs when your airways obstruct as you fall to sleep. The lack of oxygen that subsequently occurs triggers your brain to wake you up and change position to open your airway. For some people, this can occur numerous times per hour and the person cannot drop into the restorative REM (rapid eye movement) cycle of sleep. These people can sleep all night and never feel rested. This condition is diagnosed with a sleep study and is often treated by CPAP (continuous positive airway pressure).

CPAP is applied as you wear a mask, attached to a machine, that provides a continuous low flow of air to keep your airways from closing. There are also dental appliances that can be worn at night to keep your airways from closing and in some cases corrective surgery. I have had patients whose sleep apnea caused their mood disorder and once treated by CPAP were able to get off of their anti-depressants.

Sleep apnea is more common if you are overweight, over 40, or male, but I've found it in younger, thin people as well (enlarged tonsils, the shape of the jaw, deviated septum, etc.). If you toss and turn all night, don't feel rested when you wake, have restless legs, snore, or your spouse says you stop breathing, ask your medical provider to order a sleep study for you. Sleep apnea is a serious disorder. The lack of oxygen at night is very stressful to your brain and heart. People with sleep apnea are at increased risk for heart disease, hypertension, obesity, diabetes, decreased immunity, dementia, mood disorders, decreased work performance, and accidents.

Declare over yourself what David wrote years ago, "In peace I will lie down and sleep, for you alone, Lord, make me dwell in safety" (Ps. 4:8), and his son, Solomon, wrote, "When you lie down, you will not be afraid; when you lie down, your sleep will be sweet" (Prov. 3:24).

LIGHT THERAPY

Light therapy or phototherapy is a simple, safe, and inexpensive treatment for mild to moderate MDD, both seasonal and nonseasonal. Light therapy can be done at home—preferably in the early morning—and involves daily exposure to a bright light of 10,000 lux. Although the mechanism of action is unconfirmed, it is thought that light therapy works by affecting the circadian pacemaker in the brain and may also regulate the neurotransmitters serotonin and dopamine.

There is considerable evidence for light therapy as an effective treatment for seasonal affective disorder, but in a randomized clinical trial of elderly patients, light therapy was comparable to medication for treatment of nonseasonal MDD as well.[6] CANMAT recommends light therapy as first-line treatment for seasonal MDD and as an adjunctive treatment for mild to moderate nonseasonal MDD.[7]

Light therapy may also be helpful for postpartum depression, premenstrual dysphoric disorder, sleep disorders, shift work problems, and jet lag. If you are going to initiate light therapy, make sure you obtain a bright white light of 10,000 lux. Some LED lights have been shown to be as effective as bright fluorescent lights. The light needs to be large enough for you to be able to sit at a comfortable distance, and it should be projected downward, so you don't look into the light directly. Improvement of symptoms usually occurs in one to three weeks. Side effects to light therapy are usually mild, but can include eye strain, headache, agitation, and nausea.

I recommend light therapy and just getting outside for most of my patients suffering from depression. This treatment can be particularly helpful when combined with exercise. If you are struggling with a mood disorder, take a 30-minute walk or bike ride in the morning. You will be amazed at how much better you feel. You can even combine your walk or ride with prayer and meditation. What a great way to start your day, and it's good for you!

As I mentioned earlier, Jesus modeled a perfect lifestyle for us. Think about it. He ate a Mediterranean diet, which we are now recommending for most people. Exercise and light therapy were part of His daily routine, and he went to bed and slept when the sun went down. At least, He slept when He wasn't praying!

We can learn a lot from Jesus about being healthy in our spirit, our mind, and our body. The Apostle John said, *"Beloved, I pray that you may prosper in all things and be in health, just as your soul prospers"* (3 John 2 NKJV). It is not just our spiritual health that concerns God. Our physical and mental health is a priority to Him as well.

ACTION POINTS

1. Are you truly exercising 30 minutes daily at least five times per week? If not, then why?

_____

_____

_____

_____

_____

2. Pray and ask the Father for ideas and a strategy to incorporate exercise into part of your daily routine.

_____

_____

_____

_____

_____

3. Are you getting eight hours of sleep most nights? If not, why?

_____

_____

_____

_____

_____

4. What do you need to change in your routine or physical environment to create a restful environment for your brain to fall into sleep?

_____

_____

_____

_____

_____

NOTES

1. Carl W. Cotman, Nicole C. Berchtold, and Lori-Ann Christie, "Exercise Builds Brain Health: Key Roles of Growth Factor Cascades and Inflammation," *Trends in Neurosciences* 30, no. 9 (2007): 464-72, doi:10.1016/j.tins.2007.06.011.

2. James A. Blumenthal et al., "Exercise and Pharmacotherapy in the Treatment of Major Depressive Disorder," *Psychosomatic Medicine* 69, no. 7 (2007): 587-96, doi:10.1097/psy.0b013e318148c19a.

3. Ravindran, *Clinical Guidelines*, 556-557.

4. Dag Neckelmann, Amstein Mykletun, and Alv A. Dahl, "Chronic Insomnia as a Risk Factor for Developing Anxiety and Depression," *Sleep* 30, no. 7 (July 1, 2007): 873-80.

5. Dónal O'Mathúna and Walter L. Larimore, *Alternative Medicine: The Christian Handbook* (Grand Rapids, MI: Zondervan, 2001), 134-136.

6. Ritsaert Lieverse et al., "Bright Light Treatment in Elderly Patients with Nonseasonal Major Depressive Disorder," *Archives of General Psychiatry* 68, no. 1 (2011): 61-70, doi:10.1001/archgenpsychiatry.2010.183.

7. Ravindran, *Clinical Guidelines,* 555-556.

Chapter 18

Humor:
The Power of Laughter

"The arrival of a good clown exercises a more beneficial influence upon the health of a town than of twenty asses laden with drugs."
—THOMAS SYDENHAM, seventeenth-century physician

I n the last two chapters we reviewed nutrition, supplements, exercise, sleep, and light therapy as areas to optimize as we support the physical aspects of our brain. I have included humor as the last chapter in this section on physical support. Humor and laughter have a direct physical effect on the brain, causing release of chemicals that give us pleasure. Laughter alone, without humor, does this as well. We tend to overlook this area, and it's unfortunate as laughter is inexpensive and the benefits are profound.

Laughter truly is good medicine. Even as early as the thirteenth century, physicians used laughter to distract their patients during painful procedures. We now have a growing body of evidence that shows laughter and having a sense of humor is therapeutic for humans. In fact, scientists call the study of laughter gelotology, which is rather funny in itself.

We begin laughing as early as three to four months of age, which is long before we can speak or understand a joke, and on average adults laugh 17 times per day. Most laughter occurs in social situations and increases social bonding, which may explain why isolated people are more likely to experience depression.

Laugher is a bit different from other emotions that are controlled in the frontal lobe of the brain. Several regions of the brain must be involved for laughter to occur. An interesting study published in *Nature*[1] showed that a 16-year-old girl who was undergoing surgery for her epilepsy laughed every time an area in the left frontal lobe, called the frontal gyrus, was electrically stimulated. The patient was awake during this process and stated she felt a sense of merriment or mirth when she laughed, due to the electrical stimulation. She attributed it to something funny each time. The researchers felt that laughter is part of a larger area in the brain that includes the thinking part of humor (understanding a joke) and the motor part of humor (facial muscles involved in smiling). The sense of merriment the patient felt would also include activation of the emotional part of the brain. We do know that people who have experienced damage in certain areas of the brain laugh less than others.

So how does laughter work? Laughter occurs when there is an unexpected result to an event—a paradox or a surprise outcome. In a study of ten adults, using an EEG (electroencephalogram) to measure brain activity, Peter Derks, a professor of psychology at the College of William and Mary, discovered that whether or not people laughed at a joke was dependent on how quickly their brain processed the incongruity of the joke.[2] When you hear a joke, the left side of your cortex analyzes both the words and the structure of the joke. Then the frontal lobe area of your brain responsible for your emotional, social response becomes active. Meanwhile, the other side of your brain, the right cortex, intellectually works to understand the joke. Brainwave activity then spreads to the occipital (back of your brain) lobe, which is your sensory processing area. When the motor sections are stimulated, the actual physical response of laughter occurs. This electrical pattern happens in 0.4 seconds. Another researcher, Dean Shibata, MD, an assistant professor of radiology from the University of Rochester Medical Center, discovered the brain's "funny bone" with MRI scanning.[3] He discovered that while participants listened to the punch line of a joke, an area in the brain called the nucleus accumbens was activated. Once activated, the nucleus accumbens releases dopamine (a feel-good neurotransmitter) that plays a role in our processing of motivation and pleasure as well as addiction. The bottom line here is that laughter involves numerous areas of the brain, resulting in releases of neurotransmitters that give us pleasure.

Imaging of the brain has shown that people with depression have decreased activity in areas associated with pleasure. In fact, 50 percent of patients who were suffering from severe depression and underwent a treatment involving deep brain stimulation of the nucleus accumbens had a reduction in their depression and anxiety.[4] This research may open up new ways to treat people with anxiety and depression. In the meantime, using humor to activate this area of the brain and release dopamine is a good way to relieve stress and make you feel better.

Laughter temporarily increases blood pressure and heart rate, affects breathing patterns, reduces catecholamines, hormones, and boosts immunity. It is a good way for people to relax because muscle tension is reduced after laughing. There is research that shows watching funny videos can reduce pain and prevent negative stress reactions.

The emotion ascribed to laughter is mirth. Mirth, like other emotions, produces chemical changes in our brain and hormone system as described in earlier chapters of this book. Physically, mirth not only increases dopamine production, which gives us a sense of pleasure, but it also causes the brain to release endorphins, which can reduce pain.

Having a sense of humor and laughter may keep you from developing heart disease. A study by Michael Miller, MD, director of the Center for Preventive Cardiology at the University of Maryland Medical Center, found that people with heart disease displayed more anger and hostility and were 40 percent less likely to laugh compared to those without heart disease.[5] Laughter is a stress reducer, and it is suspected that this helps protect the lining of our blood vessels from inflammation that attracts fatty plaque in the coronary arteries leading to heart attacks. In addition, the after effects of laughter have been shown to lower blood pressure and increase the flow of blood through our arteries, increasing oxygenation throughout the body, similar to the effects of aerobic exercise. If you laugh 100 times, it is the equivalent of exercising 15 minutes on a stationary bike. Laughter truly is good medicine.

A joyful heart is good medicine, but a crushed spirit dries up the bones (Proverbs 17:22 ESV).

An additional benefit of laughter includes the reduction of stress. Researchers have found that people with a strong sense of humor experience less depression and anxiety when stressed compared to those who don't. Laughter also helps people cope with difficult situations in which they might feel helpless. Medical staff, myself included, use humor to relieve the tension that can build when caring for a critically ill or a difficult patient. Our humor can be a bit morbid, and others may not find it so funny, but it helps us cope. I remember a patient who tried to describe the severity of her headache. As I asked her questions, she said, "You know… it's one of those *my brain's.*" I had a hard time keeping a straight face. I've also had patients describe their cough as being in their barronicles (bronchioles) or pregnancy as a tubular (tubal) pregnancy, which makes me think of barnacles and a great surfing wave. I hope you're laughing! I have some really funny stories from working the STD clinic at the public health department, but we won't go there!

When we are under stress, our body releases chemicals and hormones that decrease our immunity and affect our sleep. Laughter can improve our ability to fight infection, ease digestion problems related to stress, improve memory and creativity, improve sleep, and promote social connection. People want to be around those who laugh. There is a pharmaceutical sales representative who comes into our office periodically. I avoid reps as much as possible, but when she comes in I come out of my office to talk to her. She makes me laugh, and I feel good for quite some time afterward. You probably know people like that as well.

A sense of humor can get us through the most difficult situations. Finding a way to laugh at our circumstances helps us survive because it alters the way we think and it renews our mind.

So does God laugh? Is God funny? Actually, God has a great sense of humor. We are created in His image. Our ability to comprehend humor and express humor through laughter is a reflection of the Father Himself. I suspect He is quite good at it, and I would be surprised if there isn't tremendous laughter in Heaven. If we enjoy laughter, how much more so does God?

In fact, creation itself portrays God's humor. There are some animals that I find ridiculous in appearance. When I see them, I spontaneously chuckle. What was God thinking when He made a blue-footed booby? Much of creation is majestic and awe-inspiring, but some of it is downright funny.

I suspect God laughs at some of our antics as well. I'm not talking about laughing in a mean way, but with genuine humor. I have a dear friend who is a believer and has the craziest things happen to him. I often beg him to repeat the stories, even though I've heard them before, because they make me laugh so hard that tears roll down my cheeks. My belief is that when God is feeling sad, there are some angels who periodically come and set my friend up so God can get a good laugh. They know my friend will take the bait. I suspect there are some people on this earth God designed just to make Him laugh.

If you spend time in God's presence, you will find yourself laughing. Many years ago when I had only been working as a nurse practitioner for a few years, I found myself comparing my skills to another nurse practitioner I admired greatly. I muttered under my breath, "I wish I could practice medicine as well as Midge." Immediately I heard the Lord say to me, "But I like the way you practice medicine." It brought me up short, and I laughed. God like the way I practiced medicine? That was rich, coming from the one who is the great physician. I said, "I like the way you practice medicine too." I could feel the Lord chuckle with me.

Humor is different for everyone. What I consider funny—*My Big Fat Greek Wedding, Napoleon Dynamite,* and *Pink Panther* movies—is far different from what my husband prefers. For the life of me I cannot comprehend what's so funny in Chevy Chase or Mel Brooks movies. To me, they are juvenile, but my husband and both of my adult sons think they are hysterical. Maybe it's a guy thing. At any rate, you need to find what's funny for you. Just Google funniest movies and books of all time and you will find an excellent selection. I suspect if you watched a funny movie every day, your mood would improve.

I've discovered some very humorous stories in the Bible. Can you imagine being talked to by a donkey (see Num. 22:28-30)? And what's even funnier in this story is that Balaam talks back to the donkey. Or how about the story of the Philistines who captured the Ark of the Covenant and placed it in their temple to Dagon? When they went into the temple the next morning, they found their idol fallen face down in front of the ark. So they set the idol up again, and the next day they found it not only fallen but the hands and head broken off (see 1 Sam. 5:1-5).

That's quite humorous when you think about it. Even Jesus had a sense of humor. Think about the story of the demon-possessed man in the Gerasenes. When Jesus cast the spirits out of the man, they entered a herd of pigs. In a full-blown panic, the pigs rushed over a steep hill and drowned in the lake. This story is humorous for a couple of reasons. What were Jews doing raising pigs? Jesus took care of that. The other funny part is that the demons begged Jesus not to send them out of the area, and He honored their request in a very literal manner. These are just a few of the many humorous incidents found in the Bible. I recommend you read the Bible with an eye to humor and see what you find. God gives laughter and joy because it's in His nature.

> *When the Lord restored the fortunes of Zion, we were like those who dreamed. Our mouths were filled with laughter, our tongues with songs of joy* (Psalm 126:1-2).

Laughter is a wonderful expression of joy, and joy is the hallmark of the believer. I encourage you to actively discover humor and laugh each day because it's God's desire for you to uncover this aspect of His nature.

ACTION POINTS

1. What do you find funny? (This can vary from person to person.)

_____

_____

_____

2. Surround yourself with funny people. Who in your life is funny? How can you spend more time with them?

_____

_____

_____

3. What can you read, watch, or listen to that will make you laugh? Make a point of laughing daily.

NOTES

1. Itzhak Fried et al., "Electric Current Stimulates Laughter," *Nature* 391, no. 650 (February 12, 1998), doi:10.1038/35536.
2. Peter Derks et al., "Laughter and Electroencephalographic Activity," *Humor: International Journal of Humor Research* 10, no. 3 (1997), doi:10.1515/humr.1997.10.3.285.
3. "Finding the Brain's Funny Bone," University of Rochester Medical Center, November 27, 2000, https://www.urmc.rochester.edu/news/story/-232/finding-the-brains-funny-bone.aspx.
4. Bettina H. Bewernick et al., "Nucleus Accumbens Deep Brain Stimulation Decreases Ratings of Depression and Anxiety in Treatment-Resistant Depression," *Biological Psychiatry* 67, no. 2 (2010): 110-116, doi:10.1016/j.biopsych.2009.09.013.
5. Michelle Murray, "Laughter Is the Best Medicine for Your Heart," University of Maryland Medical Center, July 14, 2009, http://umm.edu/news-and-events/news-releases/2009/laughter-is-the-best-medicine-for-your-heart.

Conclusion

In spite of what the world around us says, our normal state as believers in Jesus should be one of joy. Joy is our fragrance to a dying world. No matter our circumstances, joy is accessible because God Himself is full of joy and He dwells in us.

One of the key principles discussed was that feelings are valuable indicators of our thoughts but don't necessarily reflect the truth. Anxiety and depression are the fruit of our thought life and are the result of the types of trees we allow to grow in our mind. The Tree of Faith produces the fruits of the spirit and the trees of unbelief and bitterness produce rage, envy, jealousy, fear, etc. The Tree of Faith cannot thrive in the poisoned soil produced by the trees of unbelief or bitterness.

Another key point is that we are body, mind, and spirit, and anxiety and depression can be rooted in any of these three areas. Identifying the root is critical for treatment to be effective. Counseling for those struggling with a mood disorder due to a hormonal imbalance will be of limited benefit. Similarly, medication will have minimal benefit for those who are unwilling to forgive. Not all anxiety and depression have the same root, nor is any one treatment plan the same for each person.

The brain is a physical organ, and some of the supportive things we can do to optimize neural function are to consume a Mediterranean type diet, limit alcohol, consider certain supplements, exercise, sleep eight hours daily, expose ourselves to sunlight or light therapy, and laugh.

Supportive treatments that are focused toward healthy thought patterns include counseling that helps us identify lies, take our thoughts captive, forgive, set healthy boundaries, nourish our mind with good news and kind thoughts, and live in the present.

Lastly, we are spirit, and treatments oriented to this sphere include understanding our identity in Christ, wearing our God-given armor, directing our speech, remembering past victories, and being thankful. Most important of all in this category is praise and worship that brings us into the presence of God where the mind is renewed through revelation.

I encourage anyone struggling with anxiety and depression to see their medical provider to rule out physical causes, and certainly all of the tools in this book can be implemented by anyone. If the anxiety or depression is severe or is not responsive to lifestyle changes, counseling, or prayer, medications should be considered. Although not a panacea, medications, when used appropriately, can help normalize brain chemistry so that counseling and prayer become more effective. There is no shame in medical treatment or in taking medications. God brings healing to us through a variety of mechanisms and one of the tools He uses is medication.

My hope is that this book has helped you identify strongholds in your mind that are not under the Lordship of Christ and has given you practical tools to renew your mind. It's important to remember that life is a process, and some of the keys in this book may take longer to master than others. Renewing our mind to the mind of Christ is a daily journey until that day when we see Him face to face.

About Julie Winter

Julie Winter is a family nurse practitioner and currently works in private practice in Redding, California. She has a master's degree in nursing from UCLA and has 29 years of experience helping people find freedom from anxiety and depression. Julie serves on Redding City Council, and also serves on the board of her local professional organization, Advance Redding, and Bethel Church. She and her husband, Mike, have two sons and four grandchildren.

FREE E-BOOKS?
YES, PLEASE!

Get **FREE** and deeply discounted **Christian books** for your **e-reader** delivered to your inbox **every week!**

IT'S SIMPLE!

VISIT lovetoreadclub.com

SUBSCRIBE by entering your email address

RECEIVE free and discounted e-book offers and inspiring articles delivered to your inbox every week!

Unsubscribe at any time.

SUBSCRIBE NOW!

LOVE TO READ CLUB

visit **LOVETOREADCLUB.COM** ▶